THE SEALS OF WISDOM

Seek this wisdom by doing service, by strong search, by questions, and by humility; the wise who see the truth will communicate it unto thee, and knowing which thou shalt never fall into error.

SHRI KRISHNA

SACRED TEXTS

GENERAL EDITOR

RAGHAVAN IYER

This series of fresh renderings of sacred texts from the world's chief religions is an inspiring testament to the universality of the human spirit. Each text is accompanied by an instructive essay as an aid to reflection. In the ancient world, before the proliferation of print, seekers of wisdom thought it a great privilege to learn a text, and sought oral instruction from a Teacher in the quest for enlightenment. The scriptures of all traditions are guides to the attainment of serene continuity of consciousness through the practice of self-study, self-transcendence and self-regeneration in daily life.

SACRED TEXTS

THE SEALS OF WISDOM

The Seals of Wisdom is a fresh rendition of ten sections from the *Fusus al-Hikam,* a masterpiece of Sufi mystical philosophy. Its author, Muhyiddin ibn al-'Arabi (A.D. 1165-1240), offered this major treatise in his mature years as the summation of his thought. He thereafter came to be called 'the ocean of the Arabs'. Each gem of wisdom is displayed through the character of a prophet. His own preface is included together with an introductory essay, "The Current of Islam", by Professor Elton Hall. This sketches the history of Islam and the emergence of Sufi thought. A glossary of Arabic terms is included and Ibn al-'Arabi's diagram of the macrocosm is appended.

THE SEALS OF WISDOM

WISDOM

FROM THE FUSUS AL-HIKAM

MUHYIDDIN IBN AL-ʿARABI

CONCORD GROVE PRESS
1983

CONCORD GROVE PRESS
London   Santa Barbara   New York

First Printing: September 30, 1983

ISBN 0-88695-010-4

Printed in the United States of America

CONTENTS

All is contained in the Divine Breath,
As is light in the darkness before dawn.
Knowledge transmitted by proof
Is like the dawn to one half drowsing.
He perceives what we speak of as in a dream,
But that gives him a clue to the Breath.

IBN AL-'ARABI

Osiris, Krishna, Buddha, Christ, will be shown as different means for one and the same royal highway of final bliss — Nirvana. Mystical Christianity teaches *self*-redemption through one's own seventh principle, the liberated Paramatma, called by the one Christ, by the others Buddha; this is equivalent to regeneration, or rebirth in spirit, and it therefore expounds just the same truth as the Nirvana of Buddhism. All of us have to get rid of our own Ego, the illusory, apparent self, to recognise our true Self, in a transcendental divine life.

THE MAHA CHOHAN

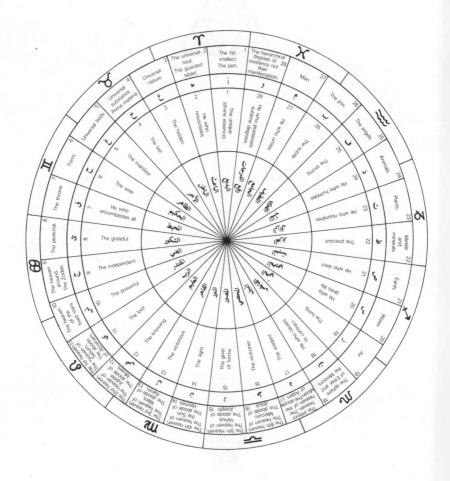

The Macrocosm
[According to Ibn al-'Arabi]

THE CURRENT OF ISLAM

The ideal and morally perfect man should be of East Persian derivation, Arabic in faith, of Iraqi education, a Hebrew in astuteness, a disciple of Christ in conduct, as pious as a Greek monk, a Greek in the individual sciences, an Indian in the interpretation of all mysteries, but lastly and especially a Sufi in his whole spiritual life.

Ikhwan as-Safa
(Brethren of Purity)

Islam as a religion, social order and way of life blends striking simplicity of faith with a subtle perspective on the cosmos, man and nature. Arising in a harsh land amongst a people who were trading nomads, Islam ignited a cultural renewal and intellectual renaissance in Egypt, Palestine, Tunisia, Spain, Persia and India within two hundred years of its birth. Although attacked in a series of indecisive crusades by Christian warriors and studiously ignored by later Christian scholars, Islam significantly contributed to the Italian Renaissance and indirectly affected the Reformation, the Elizabethan age and the rationalism of the eighteenth century. It ended the thousand-year conflict between the Mediterranean world and Persia by destroying the Byzantine Empire and conquering the Iranian plateau. Spreading into Africa, it supported the remarkable empire of Timbuktu and the trading centres of Zanzibar. In India it contributed to the exaltation of Indian music and built the Taj Mahal. And throughout its history it has ceaselessly channelled ideas from one culture to another, with the result that Europe recovered its own classical heritage from Arabic texts and Arabic numerals from Hindu India, and the East learnt of the West through Muslim traders.

Every religious tradition is subject to a tendency towards diffusion and degradation through history, almost as if according to a law of concretion and gravity. An initial spiritual impulse, wedded to the intuitive understanding of a group of individuals who recognize that life is more than living, is gradually overlaid with a filigree of institutions, practices, rituals and rules that express the evolving hopes and changing aspirations of men and women, until the original core of insight is imprisoned in the architecture intended to express it. Each religion contains its own processes of rejuvenation which involve ways to return to the essentials through renewed devotion, purified thought and cleansed action. Islam embodies the key to its vitality in its name: *islam* means 'surrender', surrender to the divine will, consecration to the deific presence in and beyond man and Nature. Muslims (from *muslimum*, 'believer') seek to make themselves sanctified instruments through nurturing a sense of the sacred in thought, speech and action. Finding a middle way between exclusive concern with individual salvation and excessive faith in the rituals of the community, they believe that spiritual life involves a consistent personal effort and the collective solidarity of awakened brotherhood.

According to Ibn Hisham's *Sirat-ar-Rasul*, the oldest account of the life of the Prophet, Muhammad was born in the year of the elephant, probably A.D. 571. Muhammad's mother, Aminah, lost her husband just before her child was born, and so even though he was part of a long-established clan which lived in Mecca, he was sent to live with Halimah, a bedouin woman of the tribe of Banu S'ad. As a nomadic shepherd, he unknowingly fulfilled the traditional Semitic belief that every prophet is a shepherd in youth. After several years amongst the wandering bedouin of Ta'if, he returned to Mecca, only to find that his mother had died. He stayed with his grandfather until the old man's death and was then raised by Abu Talib, his uncle, who gave him the rudiments of an education and trained him in the management of caravans. Whilst a youth, Muhammad travelled with his uncle in a caravan to Bostra in Syria. Along the way he met clans and tribes who worshipped *jinn*, were Jewish, Christian and perhaps Zoroastrian, and he learnt of the *hanifs*, the solitary wanderers who sought the One God of Abraham. Legend suggests that Muhammad was deeply moved by the land in which Abraham had lived, where the Mosaic Torah had been revealed, where David had composed his *Zabur* (psalms) and where Jesus proclaimed the *Injil* (evangel), the gospel or good news. In Syria, Muhammad met Bahira, a Nestorian Christian monk who declared to the youth that he would be endowed with prophecy; and, H.P. Blavatsky hinted, this encounter, in part a product of Christian strife and internecine persecution, planted the seed which flowered as Islam.

Sometime after his return to Mecca, Muhammad entered the service of Khadijah, a rich widow considerably his senior. He managed her caravans with such skill and loyalty that he became her steward and eventually her husband. They had seven children, but only the famous Fatimah survived childhood. During this period Muhammad adopted the slave Zaid ibn Harithah as his son and freed him. These contrasting qualities — an ability to be profoundly affected by sacred history, an exceptional skill in nomadic business affairs, and the compassionate love that manifested as unwavering devotion to Khadijah until her death and as fatherly love for Zaid — all grew as Muhammad matured. A turning-point was reached in his fortieth year, and he began to take up ascetic practices, including long retreats into the mountains surrounding Mecca for meditation. Always thought of as rather ethereal, he became an eccentric in a society of highly individual people. For increasingly extended periods of time he sat in caves and contemplated the spangled heavens of crystalline desert nights, and wandered across the primordial landscape searching for the key that could unlock the vault of tangled traditions in which the truth must be hidden. One night, in a niche on Mount Hira, during the month of Ramadan, he fell into a dream which was the infusion of the uncreated Word into the relative world. The Book entered the heart of the Prophet.

In Muhammad's dream a mysterious being whom he would come to know as the angel Jibra'il (Gabriel) appeared holding a scroll. "Read", the angel ordered. "I do not know how to read", Muhammad replied. "Read", the angel said again and yet again, whilst winding the scroll about Muhammad's neck. "What shall I read?" the dreamer asked in wonderment.

> Read, in the name of thy Lord who hath created,
> Who hath created man from a clot of blood.
> Read, for thy Lord is wholly beneficent.
> He hath taught man to use the pen.
> He hath taught man what man knew not.

When he awoke from this Night of Destiny, he rushed in confusion from the cave, only to discover the vault of heaven filled with the dazzling iridescence of Jibra'il's presence. In every direction he looked — in the sky, on the ground, amongst the caverns and crevices of Mount Hira — Jibra'il greeted him. Once the vision faded, Muhammad made his way towards Mecca, half convinced that he had gone mad. When he arrived home, he confided his experience to Khadijah, who soothed and supported him. Believing that the sincerity of her husband's quest protected him from demonic delusion, she insisted that he had indeed been given a divine charge. She consulted her aged cousin, Waraqah, a converted Christian, who agreed that Muhammad's mysterious visitor was the angel who had spoken to Moses and the prophets.

Muhammad was thrust out of a life of success, comfort and respect into isolation, ignominy, struggle and eventual fame as the Prophet of Allah. He left off managing caravans and turned his business over to others, devoting his time to wandering in hills and byways, seeking further revelatory enlightenment. At first no light came, and he was plunged into agonizing self-doubt. He persevered, in great part because of Khadijah's unwavering support, and in time Jibra'il spoke again. From then the divine messages came with increasing regularity, and Muhammad gained an initial confidence that became unshakeable certitude. Yet for three years, only a few intimate friends accepted the mission of Muhammad: Khadijah, his cousin 'Ali, his adopted son Zaid, and his friends Abu Bakr and 'Uthman, founder of the Umayyad dynasty. He did not dramatize the message he was receiving until he was ordered to do so in a vision, and then he confronted the Quraishites of Mecca with a fourfold message — the Oneness of Allah (from *al-illah*, the God), the need for inward repentance, accompanied by the practice of compassion, and the immanence of the last judgement.

> Everything on earth is subject to decay.
> Alone the face of the Lord remains in glorious majesty.
> Whoever does a grain's worth of good shall see it;
> Whoever does a grain's worth of evil shall also see it.

As one might have predicted, the Meccan community, accustomed to a tolerant if unformulated polytheism, did not take kindly to the fiery call for reform. Muhammad affronted their vague religious sensibilities and threatened their strict economic hierarchy and strong tribal independence. Not even his uncle, Abu Talib, who protected him throughout his troubles, surrendered to the new belief. The more openly Muhammad preached, the more hostile the chief clans in Mecca became. Many of the poor, dispossessed and enslaved were attracted, adding to the growing dislike from the established families. Avoidance turned to ridicule, then to abuse. Muslims — believers — were denied entrance to the grounds of the sacred Ka'ba, the stone cube which marked Abraham's legendary birthplace and which had long been a sacred centre for the Arabian peninsula. Whilst Muhammad had the protection of the powerful Hashemite clan, his common followers were subjected to harsh and even cruel treatment. Abu Bakr rescued a Negro named Bilal who had been stripped, tied and left to die in the sun. Because of his sonorous voice, Bilal became the first muezzin, calling the faithful to prayer. 'Ali's brother Ja'far led a small company across the Red Sea and into the protection of the Christian king of Abyssinia. In the midst of persecution, however, some intuited the depth of the message. 'Umar ibn al-Khattab, one of Muhammad's successors, joined him at this time.

The year A.D. 620 was one of tragedy for the Prophet. Abu Talib and Khadijah died. A preaching mission to nearby Ta'if was a complete failure. Yet, just as one might have thought the little band would be dispersed or extinguished, Muhammad experienced his greatest vision. In a trance he was taken on the Night Journey to Jerusalem upon the winged horse Buraq. From the ruins of the second Temple he ascended a ladder of light to the throne of heaven, passing through the nine celestial realms into the presence of the ineffable glory. After his return, relief came from the little town of Yathrib, which had chosen to follow Islam. Since Mecca had rejected the Prophet of Allah, Muhammad and his followers emigrated to Yathrib in 622. This retreat, the *hijrah*, marks the first year of the Muslim calendar. Despite religious, social and economic difficulties, Yathrib became Medina, *madinat an-nabi*, the City of the Prophet.

Here the first Islamic *umma* (community) formed, and even as it waxed, resistance in Mecca waned. At first the Meccans made forays against the Muslims and stirred up hostilities amongst the bedouin tribes in the area. Muhammad's reputation as a community leader grew, to the envy of old Medinan ruling families and the Jewish community. Though the Meccans formed a variety of subversive alliances, almost every confrontation within Medina and on the caravan routes strengthened Muhammad's position. The struggle for survival was also a holy war *(jihad)* for the sacred Ka'ba, Abraham's altar and the navel of the spiritual universe. At once practical and political, yet also visionary and mystical, previously untapped potentials — which had been made available through the electric current of caravan trade, a passionate sense of right and wrong and a tradition of compelling oral poetry — began to blossom as a vital religion of surrender and an emerging civilization that transcended old barriers of clan and tribe. The spirit of this period is perhaps best summed up in a remark Muhammad made on his return from an expedition against his Meccan foes: "We return from the lesser holy war — *jihad* — to wage the greater holy war — *mujahada"*, which is the spiritual confrontation of weakness, ignorance and imperfection within oneself.

As sometimes happens at critical points in the history of consciousness, which is the hidden history of humanity, the largest attack from Mecca was foiled by a combination of human ingenuity and seeming divine assistance. Preparing for the attack, Muhammad took the advice of Salman the Persian, who may have been a follower of Zarathustra, and ordered a great trench dug around the town. The invading army was stopped by this unexpected stratagem, and whilst the war leaders pondered their response, a capricious tornado threw the army into total disarray. Muhammad seized the initiative, routing the entire force and reducing it to slavery. Though the Quraishites would hold out for a few more years, the battle for Mecca had been won on the outskirts of Medina. Self-doubt, joined with internal disorganization and dissension, led to an agreement with Muhammad which allowed a Muslim pilgrimage to the Ka'ba in 629. Prominent Meccans converted to Islam, including General Khalid ibn al-Walid, 'Amr ibn al-'As, the future conqueror of Egypt, and al-'Abbas, Muhammad's uncle and ancestor of the Baghdad caliphs. In 630 Muhammad and his followers set out for Mecca. Abu Sufyan, the leader of the defence, allowed himself to be captured and surrendered the city after abjuring idolatry. Without a battle, they entered the precincts of the Ka'ba and overthrew the idols surrounding the sacred cube. In 632 Muhammad established the practices associated with the traditional pilgrimage to Mecca and personally delivered the sermon on Mount 'Arafat, where Adam and Eve had lived, concluding with the affirmation, "Today I have made perfect your religion." He returned to Medina, fell ill and died on June 8, 632, in the eleventh year of the Muslim calendar.

Abu Bakr was elected the first caliph or successor to Muhammad, an office designed to assure continuity in the social leadership of the *umma* without making claim to prophetic powers. The revelations that had come to Muhammad had continued throughout his life, both in Mecca and in Medina, and most of them had been written down and memorized. Abu Bakr charged Zaid ibn Thabat, Muhammad's secretary, with the responsibility of collating them. During the two years of his caliphate, he stabilized the peninsula and resolved tribal conflicts. 'Umar succeeded him by appointment, and for ten years oversaw rapid expansion and conquests. The Byzantine armies were defeated in 636 and the Persians were routed in 637 and 642, the year Alexandria fell to the Muslims. When 'Uthman became caliph in 644, he produced an authorized version of the Qur'an (recitation) and ordered all incomplete and alternative versions burnt. In this edition, chapters are organized by length from longest to shortest, and so the order in which they came to Muhammad has been lost. When 'Ali was elected caliph in 656, smouldering disagreements amongst various political and religious factions burst forth, but even as internecine warfare disturbed the emerging empire, the momentum of expansion did not slacken. Herat fell in 661, Kairouan in 670, Transoxiana in 711, Toledo in 712.

Even as Muhammad and his successors welded diverse tribes into an inchoate civilization, social and ethical differences between them — based upon unformulated intuitions of the heart — were subtly transmuted into divergent perspectives on the emerging spiritual community. The tribes of central and northern Arabia had little experience of dynastic rule, and tended towards a democracy of all adult males. Leaders were either elected by the community or emerged naturally through consensus. In both cases, qualities of leadership were associated with personal conduct. An individual earned the right to lead through demonstration of wisdom, cleverness, bravery, fortitude, and the ability to respond to the needs of the tribe or clan fair-mindedly and even-handedly. If a leader lost these qualities through weakness or indulgence, he was replaced. The southern tribes, long associated with the ancient civilization of the Yemen, were familiar with the concept of kingship. Whilst the qualities of the individual were important to them, they also believed that qualities in families were critical. The descendants of a great leader, for instance, might not display his capacities; nevertheless, it was believed, they were occultly transmitted through the family line. Thus, the descendants of a leader had a right to rule despite personal imperfections. In Islam the *umma* consists of 'the people of paradise', and the question of legitimate leadership became the question of spiritual inclusion in, or exclusion from, paradise. This difference of perspective passed through a long and complex history into the division between the Sunni and Shi'a forms of contemporary Islam.

Despite disagreements which troubled the *umma* and occasionally broke forth in violence, the roots of Islamic faith held firm. For the Muslim believer, intention *(niya)* is of fundamental importance. Where intention is conscious, consistent and sincere, observing the five Pillars of the Faith admits and keeps one in the community of believers. The chief Pillar is the repetition of the *Shahada*, 'the word of witness': *La'ilaha 'illa 'Llah, Muhammadun rasulu 'Llah*, "There is no god but Allah (one God), and Muhammad is the messenger of Allah." The remaining four Pillars are disciplines for individual growth within the solidarity of the community: *salat*, prayer, ritually performed at five appointed times each day; *zakat*, the prescribed alms, enjoined by the Qur'an, to be given to the poor; *sawm*, the fast which lasts throughout Ramadan, ninth month of the lunar year, involving total abstinence from food and drink during daylight and only light refreshment after dark; and *hajj*, the pilgrimage to Mecca, undertaken at least once in a Muslim's life if at all possible, and preferably during Dhu'l-Hijja, the twelfth lunar month. There are, of course, many other lesser ritual obligations, such as voluntary alms-giving and abstinence from alcoholic drinks and tobacco, but these five Pillars form the basis of the *umma*. Their simplicity and devotional power hold the community together in the face of internal disharmony and external adversity.

The tensions arising from incompatible perspectives manifested in a complicated and troubled history for Islam, but they opened the door to a remarkable dimension of creative expression and self-transcendence. As Muslim expansion added more peoples and territories to the *umma,* from Spain to India and eventually as far distant as Indonesia and the Philippines, the need to adjudicate questions of conduct, codify practices and unify teachings became paramount. Within three centuries the *Shari'a,* highway, was fully developed. Based on the Qur'an, which contains the whole of it in seed form, the *Shari'a* is the theory of community law, which is restricted to clarification and interpretation of divine revelation. *Shari'a* forms the basis of what might be called Islamic orthodoxy, the support and justification of simple faith, political interaction, social structure and even blind belief. At the same time, a mighty power of mystical insight, nourished by the well-springs of ascetic mysticism and expressed in ancient pre-Muslim Arabic poetry, arose in the form of small groups of disciples who sat at the feet of teachers of meditation and self-mastery. Whilst drawing apart in individual contemplation and collective aspiration, these groups continued to participate in the life of the orthodox *umma,* not denying anything whilst affirming, for those who cared to listen, a profounder interpretation of the Qur'an and a deeper level of spiritual experience. These voluntary associations of individuals who had tapped something of the hidden potentials in the human being came to be known as Sufis, at once the glorious flower of Islam and a spirit which transcended all tribes, nations, races and religions. Not so much rejecting as seeing through categories and barriers of sex, doctrine, practice and history, these 'Folk' entered the timeless company of true mystics, who press through the limitations of earthly consciousness and step across the boundaries of space and time.

The Sufi tradition can be traced to Muhammad himself. Once when he was lecturing on the Qur'anic verse "God created the seven heavens", he received a revelation in respect to its meaning. Ibn 'Abbas was amongst those present, and when he was later asked about the content of the revelation, he replied, "If I were to tell you, you would stone me to death." This remark, almost identical to the words of Thomas when asked a similar question in the *Gospel According to Thomas,* intimates the presence of an esoteric tradition amongst Muhammad's disciples. Within two centuries those who sought for the inner meaning of the teachings in light of mystical meditation were called *sufi.* Whilst some have derived the term from the Greek *sophos*, wise, and scholars believe the word is derived from the Arabic *suf*, wool — a reference to the rough woollen garments adopted by many ascetics — and yet others have connected the term with the word for 'purity', Sufis themselves hint that the word has a strictly occult origin. Whilst the nature and details of Sufi life and practice vary with the teacher, all have emphasized meditation, some degree of ascetic life, and an allegorical understanding of sacred discourse. The Batinis, as followers of esoteric interpretation were called (from *batin* — inner, occult, secret), took the Qur'an literally as a rule for the *umma* and allegorically as a spiritual guide. They easily saw beyond the parameters of doctrine into the heart of every tradition, finding sustenance in the teachings of Plato and Plotinus, the Hermetic writings, early Christian mysticism and the teachings of Vedanta and the Buddha.

The earliest characterization of the Sufi philosophy was proffered by Ma'ruf al-Karkhi, who said it consists in "the apprehension of divine realities". The gnostic and neo-Platonic spirit of *Ahl al-Haqq*, the Followers of the Real, suffuses their philosophical discourse. In the words of a Rifa'i dervish:

> Seventy Thousand Veils separate Allah, the One Reality (*al-haqq*), from the world of matter and of sense. And every soul passes before his birth through these seventy thousand. The inner half of these are veils of light; the outer half, veils of darkness. For every one of the veils of light passed through, in this journey towards birth, the soul puts *off* a divine quality; and for every one of the dark veils, it puts *on* an earthly quality. Thus, the child is born weeping, for the soul knows its separation from Allah, the One Reality. And when the child cries in its sleep, it is because the soul remembers something of what it has lost. Otherwise, the passage through the veils has brought with it *nisyan*, forgetfulness: and for this reason, man is called *insan*. He is now, as it were, in prison in his body, separated by these thick curtains from Allah.
>
> But the whole purpose of Sufism, the way of the dervish, is to give him an escape from this prison, an apocalypse of the Seventy Thousand Veils, a recovery of the original unity with the One, whilst still in this body. The body is not to be put off; it is to be refined and made spiritual — a

> help and not a hindrance to the spirit. It is like metal that
> has to be refined by fire and transmuted. And the shaikh
> tells the aspirant that he has the secret of this transmutation.
> "We shall throw you into the fire of Spiritual Passion", he
> says, "and you will emerge refined."

The Sufis, who arose in Persia and who migrated into Sind and Kashmir, linked the idea of spiritual alchemy with that of *moksha* or *nirvana*. *Fana*, the passing away of the individual self into universal Being, was joined with *baqa*, immortality in Deity. Though a goal, *fana* is also a moral state in the present — the renunciation of all passions and desires. Bayazid of Bistam declared:

> Thirty years the high God was my mirror, now I am my
> own mirror. That which I was I am no more, for 'I' and
> 'God' are a denial of the unity of the Divine. Since I am no
> more, the high God is His own mirror.
> I went from God to God until they cried from me in me,
> "O Thou I!"

Like a mighty river that flows with water from a thousand tributaries, Sufic Islam gathered the deepest mystical insights, profoundest disciplines and most ecstatic meditations into one open-textured current that surged back and forth across continents, saving, storing and sharing the best it encountered in living traditions and resurrecting the lucid fragments of a hundred broken systems.

Muslim expansion into Spain opened up new vistas of inward experience. The area, containing the artistic expression of human aspirations from the mines of the Aurignacian period (25,000 B.C.) worked for Phoenician traders, Roman frontier garrisons and the heterodox Christianity of invading Germanic tribesmen, had impressed Apollonius of Tyana with its rustic spirituality. Out of this motley collection of elements left over from the limits of dead civilizations, the Muslims forged a brilliant culture which advanced science, rejuvenated the Hellenic heritage, nurtured Jewish mysticism and built Granada and the Alhambra. Throughout Spain and North Africa, Sufi thought and practice flowered, and in Andalusia, where John of the Cross would later have his deepest experiences of the Divine Darkness, the greatest Sufi thinker was born. From the moment of his conception, Ibn al-'Arabi's life was surrounded by mysteries.

Ibn al-'Arabi's father had grown quite old without fulfilling his fondest wish: fathering a son to replace him at death. In desperation, he journeyed to Baghdad to consult the great shaikh Muhyiddin 'Abdul-Qadir Jilani and to urge him to pray for a son. Jilani retired into seclusion and entered a deep meditation. After a long time, he returned and announced: "I have looked into the world of secrets, and it has been revealed to me that you will have no descendants, so do not tire yourself out trying." The crestfallen old man beseeched the shaikh to intervene with God on his behalf. Rather than engaging in a lengthy theological discourse on the nature of destiny, Jilani once again entered into a contemplative trance. When he emerged from his reflections, he affirmed that the old man would have no descendants. But, he added, he had discovered that he himself, Jilani, was to have a son, and he offered to let his petitioner have it for him. His offer was accepted, and he ordered Ibn al-'Arabi's father to stand back to back with him, arms interlocked. Later, the old man reported:

> When I was back to back with the saint 'Abdul-Qadir Jilani, I felt something warm running down from my neck to the small of my back. After awhile a son was born to me, and I named him Muhyiddin, as 'Abdul-Qadir Jilani had ordered.

Muhyiddin ibn al-'Arabi was born Abu-Bakr Muhammad ibn 'Ali ibn Muhammad al-Hatimi al-Ta'i al-Andalusi on July 28, 1165, in Murcia, Spain. Whilst Ibn al-'Arabi occasionally spoke of particular events, his early life is not known in detail. From a very young age he exhibited a keen interest in learning and a remarkable spiritual precocity. Whilst still a child he was instructed in the Sufi Way by two elderly women who were revered for their stainless lives and mystical attainments. As a young man he travelled to Seville to study with scholars of the Qur'an, the *Shari'a* and the *hadith* (traditional sayings of Muhammad outside the Qur'an). His writings show that he also studied in depth neo-Platonic philosophy, the Hermetic tradition, alchemy and astrology. Ibn Rushd, who was known in Europe as Averroës, sought to meet Ibn al-'Arabi when the youth was nineteen years old. Ibn Rushd, famous as a rationalist philosopher, asked the young man a critical question for all aspirants to wisdom: "Do the fruits of mystic illumination agree with philosophical speculation?" Ibn al-'Arabi paused for a moment, then responded: "Yes and no. Between the Yea and Nay the spirits take their flight beyond matter." Ibn Rushd went pale in the presence of a subtle wisdom that at once reinforced his own innermost thoughts and challenged his life's work. Later, Ibn Rushd confided to friends:

> Glory to Allah that I have lived at a time when there exists a master of this experience, one of those who opens the locks of His doors. Glory to Allah that I was granted the gift of seeing one of them myself.

In addition to his studies, Ibn al-'Arabi cultivated the art of meditation. Thrice in his life he encountered Khidr, the companion of Moses and the invisible guide and prototypical teacher of all Sufis. Mystically, Khidr lives in all times and places, assisting sincere devotees to stay squarely on the Path. The highest Sufic privilege is to be made the disciple of this spiritual master. The first meeting occurred in a dream. Ibn al-'Arabi had disagreed with his teacher, Shaikh 'Abdul Hassan, over some points of doctrine. Whilst he was sleeping late that night, Khidr appeared to the dreamer, saying, "The things that your teacher told you were right — accept them." Ibn al-'Arabi awoke with a start and rushed in the middle of the night to his teacher. Whilst he was breathlessly explaining his dream, the shaikh showed no surprise. He explained that he had appealed to Khidr in meditation to correct his brilliant but stubborn student. "On hearing that," Ibn al-'Arabi later wrote, "I once and for all decided never to disagree again."

The second encounter took place during a visit to Tunisia. Ibn al-'Arabi was staying aboard ship but found one evening that he could not sleep. As he paced the deck, he noticed a figure walking across the water towards him. Khidr walked up to the edge of the boat and talked briefly with the stunned disciple. When Khidr left, he disappeared over the horizon of the sea in three steps. Ibn al-'Arabi never revealed the contents of that conversation, but he recorded that whilst he was walking through the streets of Tunis the next morning, an old shaikh came up to him and asked how his meeting with Khidr had gone. The third meeting occurred in an Andalusian mosque where Ibn al-'Arabi was lecturing on the function of creative imagination in so-called miracles. Several of those listening rejected the idea that the purified human mind could work wonders. Khidr entered unrecognized by all save Ibn al-'Arabi and rolled out his prayer mat. Suddenly he rose sixteen feet into the air and said his prayers from that altitude. The *salat* finished, he drifted slowly to the floor and left. Thus ended the debate on the creative powers of the human mind.

Ibn al-'Arabi attended the funeral of Ibn Rushd and wrote the haunting lines: "This is the *imam* (leader) and these his works; would that I knew whether his hopes were realized." About 1200 he journeyed to Marrakesh and there received the call to go to the East. Around this time his urge to communicate to others what he had learnt in the sacred sanctuary of the soul matched his will to plumb the depths of meditation. Books, essays, commentaries poured forth in amazing profusion. He himself recorded two hundred and fifty-one works, from short essays to the massive *Al-Futuhat al-Makkiyyah (Meccan Revelations)*, the printed edition of which consists of twenty-five hundred pages. In Marrakesh he was told in a vision to go to Fez, where he would meet a certain Muhammad al-Hasar, who would accompany him east. The meeting occurred as promised, and the two companions went to Bijayah and Tunis, and quickly passed on to Alexandria and Cairo, where al-Hasar died. Alone, Ibn al-'Arabi continued on to Mecca, where he had the culminating experience of his life. He met the wise Abu Shaja Zahir ibn Rustam, who warmly welcomed him into a small company of learned men and women. Ibn al-'Arabi wrote:

> This shaikh had a virgin daughter, a slender child who captivated all who looked on her, whose presence gave lustre to gatherings, and who amazed all she was with and ravished the senses of all who beheld her. . . . She was a sage amongst the sages of the Holy Places.

Inspired by her radiant presence and tranquil wisdom, Ibn al-'Arabi found in her Plato's Diotima and anticipated Dante's Beatrice, who may have been partly modelled on this Meccan Hypatia. In about 1215 he completed his *Tarjuman al-Ashwaq (Interpreter of Desires)*, a collection of mystical odes in the form of love poems reminiscent of the *Song of Songs* and some Krishna *bhajans*. Their *eros*, creative power and sensuous texture scandalized the orthodox scholars, and he felt compelled to compose a commentary upon them.

Whilst in Mecca, Ibn al-'Arabi received two initiations, the contents of which he never revealed in detail. The first was a vision of the Eternal Youth, who fuses in himself all pairs of opposites. The second confirmed him as the Seal of the Saints. In 1204 he travelled to Baghdad and then Mosul, where he received a third initiation and wrote his *Mosul Revelations*. He returned to Cairo in 1206, only to find orthodox scholars openly hostile to him, and he was saved from arrest and probable execution by the timely intervention of a Tunisian friend who had the ear of the Ayyubid ruler of Egypt. He sought refuge in the appreciative society of Mecca, and then travelled to Aleppo and Konya. Here he was formally honoured by the king Kay Kaus, who gave him an elegant villa as a present. Ibn al-'Arabi gave the house as alms to a beggar, and soon all Konya fell in love with Ibn al-'Arabi. His chief local disciple, Sadr al-Din al-Qunawi, wrote commentaries on his works, and years later sat at the feet of Jalaluddin Rumi, bringing together the ideation of the greatest Arabic and Persian Sufis. After a sojourn that took him to the borders of Armenia, back to Mecca, and to Aleppo, he accepted an invitation to reside in Damascus. From 1223 until his death in November 1240, he stayed there as a teacher and writer. During this period of semi-retirement he composed his poetic *Diwan* and the *Fusus al-Hikam, The Seals of Wisdom*, a mature summation of his mystical philosophy.

For Ibn al-'Arabi the touchstone of vision, philosophy and daily life is *wahdat al-wujud*, the Oneness of Being. This sublime unity must be experienced to be understood — and it is the heart of all knowledge — but the illusions which can deceive the novice are immense. In his *Meccan Revelations* he declared:

> Knowledge of mystical states can only be had by actual experience, nor can the reason of man define it, nor arrive at any cognizance of it by deduction, as is also the case with knowledge of the taste of honey, the bitterness of patience, the bliss of sexual union, love, passion or desire, all of which cannot possibly be known unless one is properly qualified or experiences them directly.

The Oneness of Being is the 'seamless garment' behind all differentiation and manifestation. Oneness of Being implies a correlative Oneness of Perception, gained through a contemplative withdrawal from the senses and concentration upon the core of one's being, which is consubstantial with Being. Oneness of Perception is the direct experience of *al-haqq*, the Real. Hence, Sufis are *Ahl al-Haqq*, Followers of the Real, a term with much the same meaning that 'philosopher' had for Pythagoras.

Al-haqq is of such transcendent reality that It cannot even be called Allah, since to speak of the Divine implies that which is not divine, and even this subtle dualism does not exist in the Real as the Absolute. Yet in the sense of Its necessary omnipresence, within It is found the dance of polarity, the drama of self-consciousness which bifurcates reality into subject and object. At the highest level of the Real, where Being and Perception are one, in the condition known as *satchidananda* amongst the Hindus, self-consciousness is awareness of all as the Self, or of nothing save the Self, which is the Real, the state called *svasamvedana.* With polarization in consciousness, subject and object arise, obscuring the primordial unity of Being and Perception. The whole cycle of existence is the progressive realization of the illusory relations between the myriad mirrorings of the Real within Itself. The immediate practical conclusion, which constitutes the ethical basis of life, is that until one can see Allah manifest in everything, one will not experience the Real.

The chief power which makes possible polarization in the Real and also dissolves it is *al-khayal,* creative imagination. *Al-khayal* is the link between the Real as Perceiver and the Real as object of perception. It is also illusion insofar as it can be distinguished, for all is the Real. *Al-khayal* is reminiscent of the creative power of *maya* ascribed to Krishna in the *Bhagavad Gita.* Creative imagination, the source of all creation, is archetypal self-alienation, which might be likened to the passionate act of physical love. The union of two people in physical ecstasy is at once a kind of transcendence which also reaffirms their separateness from one another on the level of their union. Lasting union must be found on a higher level, a vertical rather than horizontal creativity. Creative imagination in action is *rahmah,* compassion, a term which, according to Ibn al-'Arabi, derives from *rahima,* womb. Nothing exists save for this compassion, a kind of giving birth that contains in the act of manifestation the seed of longed-for complete reunion, *rahim*. Whilst divine Self-consciousness is self-subsistent, the upward and downward movement of *al-khayal* results in an ordinary human identity that is other-related. Thus, the human being is both the microcosm of the macrocosm and an enigmatic illusion.

Once *al-haqq*, the Real, is polarized — an act of consciousness and not an event in time — it is Allah. Polarization is the architectonic mode of the cosmos, and Allah is the Supreme Name that contains all other names and attributes. Allah is Deity as contrasted with creation, but *Rabb*, Lord, is Deity in respect to Man. Allah is the divine pen that inscribes the tablet of universal nature, *Rabb* the pulse of the human heart. If one forgets that man as the microcosm is ultimately one with the Real, one will fall into a deterministic view of cosmic activity. To counter this tendency, Ibn al-'Arabi distinguished between *al-mashi'ah* and *al-iradah*, the will and the wish. The will establishes the parameters of compassion, that is, creates the universe, without regard for faith or ethics, since this is the actuality of the cosmos, the divine geography from which ethical longitudes and latitudes are derived. The wish, on the other hand, requires that universal truths be recognized and embodied. From the human standpoint, the will concerns what is, the wish aims for reintegration with the Divine. Thus, the will is the existential pole of reality and the wish is the sapiential pole. In the Iranian theosophy of light, the Sufi journeys towards the Real by turning towards the North Pole (the wish), corresponding to the head, which is also a turning towards the East, corresponding to the dawning of light in the heart.

Ibn al-'Arabi generated analogous concepts to explicate the nature of human action. There is *qada'* and *qadar*, decree and destiny. Decree encompasses what shall irrevocably be, and destiny embraces the timing. The Divine Names, of which Allah is the highest, are the supreme archetypes, unmanifest in themselves, but manifesting in embodiments or actualizations as things and beings. Nothing is just what it is; everything is at its core the seed of an archetype or Name. Decree gives the archetype, whilst destiny is its timely unfoldment in embodied existence. Since the human being is a microcosm involved in the temporal process of unfoldment, each individual shares in divine free will. Free will in the cosmos is a philosophic problem only because it cannot be understood outside of direct experience of Deity. Thus, in man one sees both divine occultation — the Mystery of the Real hidden in the seventy thousand veils of illusion — and divine Self-manifestation — *tajalli*, theophany. The human being embodies the two poles of the Real and is the bridge between the purely divine and spiritual on the one hand, and the animal nature on the other. Man is both spirit and matter, the fulcrum of divine manifestation and reintegration.

One sees this most clearly in the Perfect Man. The Perfect Man is *barzakh*, the Isthmus or Bridge, but a bridge is significant only in that it links two things. Man is, therefore, nothing in himself, a naught. God is all. Nevertheless, within the transcendental context of God, man is the microcosmic experience of the Real. Since the Perfect Man combines in himself heaven and earth, Being and Perception, he is the eye by which the Divine sees Himself. Man is the polished mirror that reflects the Divine Light. Each human being, therefore, participates in *al-khayal*, creative imagination, at two levels. Involved in the cosmic processes of life and death, this participation is mostly instinctual, but human beings also exhibit at some rudimental level *al-himmah*, the conscious power of impressing images and ideas on the cosmos. When this power is raised through concentration and knowledge to the highest level, it becomes the pure channel of the divine creative imagination. For vast multitudes of human beings, *al-himmah* does not go beyond fantasy and daydream, but for men and women of meditation, subjective ideas can be transformed into objective reality. *Al-himmah* intensified and focussed to this degree is the cause of so-called miracles, such as that performed by Khidr in Andalusia. Ibn al-'Arabi warned that such power is also the source of malevolent magic for those who tread this Path without purging themselves of residues of egotism or travel too far without the guidance of a real teacher. The Perfect Man is that rare being who has realized the full potential of the human estate, which is the complete embodiment of the archetype.

A human being who has attained this exalted goal is called a *wali*, saint, for he has become a friend of God, one of whose names is *al-wali*, the Friend. For Ibn al-'Arabi true universal Islam is nothing other than the experience of the *wali*. All religions are particular yet partial manifestations of universal Islam. The *wali's* friendship is annihilation of otherness, total absorption in Oneness, the perfectly polished mirror, a zero in itself, though reflecting without loss *an-nur*, the Light. Such a friend may acquire the special functions of *nabi*, the prophet who has knowledge of the Unseen, or *rasul*, the messenger with a specific mission to a particular community. From an absolute standpoint — that of the Real — the idea that one must go to Mecca or even that one must tread the spiritual Path is an illusion, because the idea that one is somehow separate from the Real is an illusion. For those caught up in this root ignorance, the complex doctrine of states and stages, phases and degrees, of prophets and messengers and saints, is quite necessary. Those who do not directly experience the Real as yet can nevertheless do so indirectly through Its reflections. Thus, the Qur'an says, "Wherever you turn, there is the face of Allah." If the Real is in any sense perfect, it must contain all possibilities, including possibilities of imperfection. For Ibn al-'Arabi the glorious and awesome complex of the cosmos with all its suffering and fascination is a fleeting opportunity to seize upon the possibility in which God and Man are One.

Each prophet and messenger has witnessed this sacred possibility. Each spoke in the language available and addressed the understanding of the people, and so timeless Truth appears in history as progressively unfolding revelation. Each prophet, with his own potentials and limitations, has been a setting, a seal, for the gem of wisdom which shines forth the Divine Light. The gem is contained in and set off by the setting. When summarizing his mystical teachings, Ibn al-'Arabi chose this metaphor as the title of his work, *Fusus al-Hikam, The Seals of Wisdom*, to show the bright thread of spiritual continuity that weaves its way through the ancient prophets, the thread which is true Islam, the inner wisdom of all traditions and philosophies. In one of his love poems he caught the essence of his teaching when he wrote:

> My heart has become capable of every form;
> It is a pasture for gazelles and a convent for Christian monks,
> And a temple for idols and the pilgrim's Ka'ba
> And the tables of the Torah and the book of the Qur'an.
> I follow the religion of Love: whatever way
> Love's camels take, that is my religion and my faith.

The powerful current of Ibn al-'Arabi's thought struck the hearts of those who heard him. Many loved him and some became true disciples. Others were terrified and some violently hostile. After his death in 1240 at Damascus, the latter held the field for a time.

Ibn al-'Arabi's tomb was destroyed after his death. As if in anticipation of this sacrilege, he had once said, "When the Arabic letter *sin* enters the Arabic letter *shin*, the tomb of Muhyiddin will be found." When in 1516 the Ottoman sultan Selim II conquered Damascus, the scholar Zembilli Ali Efendi approached him and pointed out that Selim's name began with *sin* whilst Sham (the Arabic name of Damascus) began with *shin*. Selim asked the theologians what statement uttered by Ibn al-'Arabi had caused the violent reaction. When he was told that it was "The god you worship is under my feet", Selim asked to be shown the place whence Ibn al-'Arabi had spoken it. He had the spot excavated and uncovered a hoard of gold coins, thus showing Ibn al-'Arabi's ironic meaning. Nearby, he located the desecrated tomb, and with the treasure built a shrine and mosque on the site. It stands today in Damascus on Mount Qasiyun. Those who appreciated the message of Ibn al-'Arabi lost the tomb but gained the day, and he is honoured amongst Sufis and other Muslims as *al-shaikh al-akbar*, the greatest shaikh, as *qutb al-arifin*, the axis of true knowledge, and as *rahbar ul-'alam*, guide of the world. Humble as a disciple of Khidr, confident in his instruction of others and always willing to learn, this God-intoxicated mystic taught that all doctrine and practice could be found distilled in one phrase from the Qur'an:

Whoso knoweth himself, knoweth his Lord.

Traditional cosmology does not only concern the macrocosm but also the microcosm. It contains a complete knowledge of the soul as it does of the qualitative aspect of the Universe. Not only are there the earth, the seven heavens and the outermost heaven leading to the Metacosmic Reality, but there are also within man beside the physical body, the seven subtle organs or bodies *(lata'if)* which like the seven planets correspond to the various prophets of man's inner being and the centre of the heart which, like the outermost heaven, is called the *'arsh al-rahman* (the Throne of the Compassionate) wherein resides the Divinity. The contemplation of the external cosmos is an aid to the penetration of the inner world thanks to the correspondence and analogy which bind them together. As metaphysics is the key to the understanding of cosmology, so is initiation the key which opens to man the door to the inner chambers of his own being. By means of the initiatic path man enters ever more deeply within himself and at the same time through the higher levels of cosmic reality toward the Formless. His inner transformation includes the interiorization of the cosmic within his being and his freedom therefore embraces the deliverance of nature from the limitations imposed by cyclic conditions and its re-statement into its original state *in divinis* where nature is perennially a direct image of paradise.

SEYYED HOSSEIN NASR

THE SEALS OF WISDOM
FROM THE *FUSUS AL-HIKAM*

PREFACE

In the name of God, the Compassionate, the Merciful.
Praise be to God who has transmitted Wisdom through the
hearts of the Logoi, *uniquely and directly, from the Station of
Eternity, although sects and communities vary because of the
vagaries of nations. May God bless and guard him who garners
aspirations from the storehouse of abundance and munificence,
Muhammad and his family.*

I saw the Messenger of God in a vision granted me late in the
month of Muharram in the year 627, within the city of Damascus.
He held a book in his hand and he said to me, "This is the book of
the Seals of Wisdom. Take it and give it to men that they might
benefit from it." I replied, "All obedience is due to God and His
Messenger; it shall be as we are commanded." I therefore fulfilled
the wish, purified my intention and consecrated my purpose to
the presentation of this volume as the Messenger had instructed,
without addition or depletion. I pray that, in this and in everything,
He might number me amongst those of His servants over whom
Satan has no authority. And I pray, in all my hand may pen, in all
my tongue may plead, and in all my heart may veil, that He might
favour me with His deposition, His spiritual inspiration, for
protective support of my mind, that I may be a transmitter and
not a composer. Those amongst the Sufis who read it know that it
comes from the Station of Sanctification and that it is entirely free
from all the purposes of the lower soul which always aim to
deceive. I hope that the Real, having heard my supplication, will
heed my call, for I have not taught anything here save what was
set before me, nor have I written in this book anything other than
what was revealed to me. I am neither prophet nor messenger, but
merely an heir, preparing for what is to come.

> It is from God, listen!
> And to God do you return.
> When you hear what
> I bring, learn.

Then with understanding see details by the whole
And see them as parts of the totality.
Then give it to those
Who seek it, generously.
This is the Compassion that
Encompasses you; therefore expand it.

I hope to be amongst those who receive and accept aid, amongst those bound by the pure Law of Muhammad, who volunteer themselves to be bound and by it bind. May God gather us with Him as He has constituted us His Community.

IBN AL-'ARABI

DIVINE WISDOM IN THE WORD OF ADAM

Al-Hikmat al-Ilahiyah

The Real, *al-haqq*, wished to perceive the essences of His Most Beautiful Names, *al-asma al-husna*, infinite in number, or put another way, to see His own Essence in a universal medium encompassing the Divine Order, which, being qualified by existence, could reveal His mystery, *sirr*, to Himself. For the vision, *ru'ya*, of a thing unto itself is not the same as seeing itself in another, as in a mirror; for it appears to itself in a form that arises from the locus of the vision. That would only appear to it owing to the existence of the locus and its reflection shown therein.

The Real first gave existence to the entire Cosmos as homogeneity without Spirit in it, being like an unpolished mirror. The nature of Divine Creativity necessitates that no locus be prepared, save to receive a divine spirit, which is also called *the breathing into him*. The latter is nothing other than the awakening of the undifferentiated form's predisposition to receive the inexhaustible afflatus, *al-fayd*, of Self-unveiling, *at-tajalli*, which has always been and will ever be. There is only the pure receptacle, *qabil*, and the receptacle comes from the Holy Afflatus, for all Order, *amr*, derives from Him, even as it returns to Him. Thus the Divine Order required the pure reflectivity of the mirror of the Cosmos, and Adam became the light of that mirror and the spirit of the form, whilst the angels represent certain potencies of that which is the form of the Cosmos, called in the language of the Sufis, *al-insan al-kabir*, the Great Man. The angels are to it as the psychic and physical properties are to the human form. Each of these cosmic potencies is veiled by its own nature so that it cannot know anything superior to itself. Each claims that it is worthy of an exalted position and ultimate closeness to God by virtue of its participation in *al-jam-'iyat al-ilahiyah*, the Divine Synthesis, deriving both from the Sphere of Divinity and *haqiqat al-haqaiq*, the Reality of Realities, and again, with respect to the form assuming these characteristics, from the exigencies of *tabi'at al-kull*, the Universal Nature, which embraces all the receptacles of the Cosmos, higher and lower.

This cannot be comprehended by discursive logic, for this type of knowledge comes only through Divine Intuition. Through it alone one knows the origin of the forms of the Cosmos to the degree they receive the spirits. This form is called *insan* and *khalifah*, Man and the Representative of God. The first quality stems from the universality of his nature and the fact that he embraces all the realities. Man is to the Real as the pupil is to the eye through which the act of seeing takes place. Thus he is called *insan*, meaning both Man and pupil, for it is through Man that the Real contemplates His creation and bestows mercy. Thus is Man transient and eternal, perpetual, everlasting, the discriminating and unifying Word. Through his existence the Cosmos subsists. He is, in relation to the Cosmos, as the seal is to the ring, for the seal is the place where the token is engraved with which the king seals his treasure. So he is called the Representative, for through him God preserves creation, as the seal preserves the king's treasure. So long as the king's seal is on it, no one dares to open it except by permission, the seal being the safeguard of the kingdom. Even so is the Cosmos preserved so long as *al-insan al-kamil*, the Universal Man, abides in it. You see that when he shall cease to be and when the seal of the lower world is broken, nothing of what the Real preserved will persist and all of it will disperse, each part returning to its source, and the whole will be translated to the Final Abode where the Universal Man will be the seal forever.

All the Names constituting the Divine Form are manifest in the human constitution so that it encompasses and integrates all existence. From this fact comes the argument that God condemned the angels. Remember that God warns you by the example of another, and consider carefully from whence the arraigned one is judged. The angels did not grasp the meaning of the establishment of God's Representative, nor did they apprehend the essential servitude implied by the Plane of Reality. For none knows anything of the Real save that of Himself which is implicit in the Essence. The angels do not enjoy the integral nature of Adam, and they comprehend only those Divine Names peculiar to them by which they glorify and sanctify the Real; nor do they know that God has

Names of which they are ignorant and by which they cannot glorify Him. They are unable to sanctify Him with the sanctification of Adam. Their nature and limitation being such, they said, concerning Adam's constitution, *Will You put in it one who will work mischief in it?* They meant his rebellion, which is precisely what they themselves manifest, for what they say of Adam applies equally to their own attitude towards the Real. But for the fact that rebellion is in their own constitution, they would not have thus spoken concerning Adam; but they are not aware of this. If they indeed knew themselves, they would know their limitation, and if that were so, they would have restrained their speech. They would not have followed their challenge by calling attention to their own glorification of God or their sanctification. Adam partakes of Divine Names the angels have no part in, and they are not able to glorify Him to exalt His transcendence, as Adam does.

God explains this to us so that we might be careful and learn from it the right attitude towards Him, lest we become pretentious because of the individually restricted insight or understanding we might have realized. How can we possess something, the reality of which we have not experienced and concerning which we have no knowledge? This Divine Instruction is one of the ways by which the Real teaches His most trusted servants, His Representatives.

Let us now return to this Wisdom. Know that the universal ideas, *al-umar al-kulliyah*, have no tangible, individual existence in themselves. Nevertheless, they are present and known in the mind. They are always unmanifest with respect to individual existence, yet impose their effects on all such existence. In truth, individual existence is nothing other than universal ideas, though in themselves they are purely intelligible. They are manifest as individual beings, and they are unmanifest as intelligibles. Every individual existence emanates from universal ideas which can never be dissociated from the intellect, nor can universal ideas manifest individually in such a way that they would cease to be intelligible. Whether the individual being is determined in or out of time, its relationship to the universal idea remains the same. The universal idea and the individual being may share a common determining principle if the essential realities of the individual beings demand, as, for example, in the relationship between knowledge and the knower, or life and the living. Life and knowledge are intelligible realities, distinct from one another. Thus, concerning the Real, we say that He has life and knowledge and also that He is Living and Knowing. This we also say of Man and the angels. The reality of knowledge is one, and the reality of life is also one, and the relationship of each respectively to the knower and the living is always the same.

We say that knowledge of the Real is eternal, but that man's knowledge is ephemeral. Attachment to the determinant renders something in the intelligible reality contingent. Now consider the interdependence of universal ideas and individual existences. For, even as knowledge constitutes one who uses it as being a knower, so also does the knower constitute knowledge as being ephemeral in the case of the ephemeral knower, and as eternal in the case of the Eternal, each constituting and being constituted in turn. Universal ideas are intelligible, but have no real existence except insofar as they determine existing beings, just as they themselves are determined in any relationship with individual existence. As manifest in individual existence, they may admit of being determined, but it is impossible for them to admit of particularization or division. They are essentially present in each thing they qualify, just as humanity is present in every human being, whilst not being subject to particularization or division by the number of individual beings, but remaining purely intelligible.

Since there is a mutual dependence between that which has individual existence and that which has not, being but an unmanifested relationship, the interconnection between one individual being and another is the more comprehensible because they have, at least, individual existence in common, whereas in the former instance there is no common denominator. Without doubt, the ephemeral is utterly dependent for its possibility on that which brings it about. Its existence is derived from something other than itself, the connection in this case being one of dependence. It is therefore necessary that that which is the principle of ephemeral existence should be essentially and necessarily subsistent, self-sufficient and independent of all else. This principle bestows existence from its own essential being on ephemeral existence and in this way becomes related to it. Furthermore, since the principle, because of its essence, requires the ephemeral, the latter has a kind of necessary being. And since its dependence on that from which it was manifested is implicit in its own essence, it follows that the ephemeral should conform to all the Names and attributes of the origin except that of Self-sufficient Being, which does not belong to ephemeral existence, since even what necessary being it has comes from other than itself.

If the ephemeral manifests the form of the Eternal, then it is clear that God draws our contemplation towards what is ephemeral as an aid to knowledge of Him. He says that He shows forth His signs in the ephemeral. Knowledge of Him is inferred from knowledge of ourselves. Whatever quality we ascribe to Him, we ourselves represent that quality, except the quality of Self-sufficient Being. Since we know Him through ourselves and from ourselves, we attribute to Him all we attribute to ourselves, and for this reason the revelation comes to us through the mouths of the Interpreters (the prophets). He depicts Himself to us through ourselves. If we contemplate Him we contemplate ourselves, and when He contemplates us He contemplates Himself.

Obviously, as individuals and types, we are multitudinous, though representatives of a single reality. But we also know that there is a factor distinguishing one individual from another, without which there would be no multiplicity in the One. In the same way, even if descriptions of ourselves apply equally to Him in every respect, there is nevertheless a fundamental difference — we are originated in conformity to Him, and He is Being, free from all dependence. Thus, we should understand the One without beginning, *al-azal*, the Ancient of Days, *al-qidam*, denying Divine Primacy, in the sense of existence coming from non-existence. For although He is the First, *al-awwal*, no temporality may be attributed to Him, and thus He is called also the Last, *al-akhir*. If He were the First in the sense of being the first in time, He would also be called the Last in this sense, but manifestation has no end, being inexhaustible. He is called the Last only in the sense that all reality, though reality is attributed to us, returns to Him. His Finality is essentially His Primacy, and His Primacy is essentially His Finality. Know also that the Real has depicted Himself as being the Outer, *al-zahir*, and the Inner, *al-batin*, Manifest and Unmanifest. He brought the Cosmos into being as an unseen realm and a sensory realm so that we might perceive the Inner through our own interior and the Outer through our own sensory aspect.

He has also attributed to Himself mercy and wrath, having

manifested the Cosmos as a place of fear and hope, where we fear His wrath and hope for His mercy. He has also depicted Himself as being possessed of majesty and beauty, having endowed us with reverent awe, *al-haybah*, and intimacy, *al-uns*, and so on with all His attributes and Names. He has expressed this polarity of qualities as being His two Hands devoted to the creation of the Universal Man, who integrates in himself all cosmic realities and their individual manifestations.*

The Cosmos is the sensory realm, and the Representative is unseen. For this reason the Ruler is veiled, since the Real has described Himself as being hidden behind veils of darkness, which are the natural forms, and behind veils of light, which are the subtle spirits.† The Cosmos consists of *kathif* and *latif*, gross and subtle matter. It is therefore the veil covering its own reality. For the Cosmos does not perceive the Real as He perceives Himself, nor can it ever unveil itself, even though knowing itself to be distinct from its Creator, *al-khaliq*, and dependent on Him. Indeed, the Cosmos has no share in the essential Self-sufficiency of the Real, nor will it ever attain to that. In this sense the Real remains ever unknown in every way, since ephemeral being has no grasp of the Eternal.

God unites the polarity of qualities only in Adam, to confer a distinction upon him. He says to Iblis,‡ *What prevents you from prostrating to one whom I have created with my two hands?* What prevents Iblis is the very fact that man unites in himself the two forms, the ephemeral Cosmos and the Real, which are His two Hands. As for Iblis, he is only a fragment of the Cosmos and has

---

* Mercy and fear are the two poles of the Qabbalistic Tree of Life, named after the fourth and fifth Sephiroth, Chesed (mercy) and Geburah (fear). Mercy is connected with Chokhmah (wisdom), and fear derives from Binah (intelligence). They are balanced in Malkhuth (the kingdom) and in Kether (the crown), the grossest and most subtle extremities of manifestation. The polarities are synthesized in Adam Kadmon, the Cosmic Man, whose embodiment is the visible Cosmos and whose symbol is the caduceus. Ibn al-'Arabi was born and grew up in regions that nurtured the Qabbalistic *Zohar* to full flower.

† Muhammad the Prophet said, "God hides Himself in seventy thousand veils of light and darkness. If He lifted them, the brilliance of His Visage would consume whomsoever looked upon It."

‡ Iblis, the Islamic tempter, Satan.

no share in this Synthesis, by virtue of which Adam is the Representative. Were Adam not manifest in the form of Him whom he represents, he would not be the Representative, and were he not to contain all that his flock needs or were he unable to meet all the requirements of the other creatures, he would not be the Representative. Such Representation is suitable only for the Universal Man. The outer form of Universal Man is composed of all cosmic realities and forms, whilst his inner form is composed to correspond to the form of the Real. Thus He says in the Sacred Tradition (hadith), *I am his hearing and his sight*, and not, "I am his eye and his ear", in order to show the distinction between these two forms. The reality in every being in the Cosmos is in accordance with the requirements of the essence of each being, but it must be understood that no other being enjoys the Synthesis possessed by the Representative. It is by virtue of this Synthesis that he surpasses all other beings.

If the Real did not pervade all beings as form, and if there were no universal ideas, there would be no manifestation of individual beings. Thus in truth, the Cosmos depends on the Real for its existence.

> All is dependent, naught is independent,
> This is pure truth, plainly and without metaphors.
> If I mention One, Self-sufficient, Independent,
> You know I refer to the Real.
> Each is bound up with the other without break.
> Consider carefully this which I tell thee.

You are now acquainted with the Wisdom involved in the bodily form of Adam, his ephemeral form, and you are acquainted with the spiritual form of Adam, his inner form. Adam is, then, the Real, and he is a creature. You have also learnt to know his rank as the Synthesis by virtue of which he is the Representative.

Adam is that single soul, that single spiritual essence, *an-nafs al-wahidah*, from which humankind was created, as the Real proclaims in the Qur'an: *O Men, fear your Lord who created you from a single soul and created from it its mate, so that from them both there issued forth many men and women*. The words *Fear your Lord* mean, make your ephemeral selves a safeguard for your Lord and make your inner reality, which is your Lord, a safeguard for your ephemeral selves. The Divine Order, *amr*, involves blame and praise, negation and affirmation; so be His shield in censure and make Him your safeguard in praise, so that you belong to those who act justly and are possessed of knowledge.* The Most High and Glorious caused Adam to look on all He had placed in him and held it in His Hands, the Cosmos in one Hand and in the other Adam and his seed, expounding their degrees in the inner Adam.

When God unveiled to me, in my innermost centre, what He had placed in our primordial ancestor, I set down in this volume only that which was shown to me, though not all I was given, since no book could hold it all, nor could the Cosmos as it presently exists. The seal of each Wisdom is the Word unveiled in it. I have transcribed faithfully according as was vouchsafed to me. Even if I wished to add to it, I would not be able to do so, since the plane from which it came prevents saying more.

---

* The Qur'an (IV, 81) says: "Whatsoever good befalleth thee is from God; whatsoever evil comes to thee is from thyself."

THE WISDOM OF INSPIRATION IN THE WORD OF SETH

Al-Hikmat an-Nafathiyah

Know that the divine gifts and graces which manifest in the realm of ephemeral being, whether through mediation of His servants or not, are divided into two kinds in the sight of men of spiritual inclination *(adh-dhawq)*: gifts of the Essence and gifts of the Names. There are gifts given in answer to a specific request and gifts resulting from a general request. There are also gifts that are bestowed without any request, whether deriving from the Essence or the Names. An example of a request for something specific is one such as, "O Lord, *Rabb*, grant to me such and such", naming something to the exclusion of anything else. An example of a general request is one such as, "Grant to me what You know to be in my interest, whether for my subtle or physical being."

Those who ask can be divided into two kinds: the first asks in obedience to a natural eagerness for attainment, since *Man was created hasty*. The second kind asks knowing that there are certain things near God that cannot, according to Divine Foreknowledge, be obtained save by asking. This kind says, "Perhaps what we are about to ask for is of this kind." His request includes a global awareness of the possibilities inherent in the Divine Order. He cannot know what is in the Divine Science, and he does not know his own predisposition *(isti 'dad)* to receive, for it is most difficult to know one's predisposition at each instant. In fact, without the predisposition, he would not make the request at all. For those meditating and who do not usually know this, the most they attain to is recognition of the predisposition when receiving or asking. Because of their presence with God, they know what the Real gives them at any time, and they know that they receive it only because of their predisposition. They are of two kinds: those who know their predisposition by recognizing what they receive, the others knowing what they receive by recognizing their predisposition. This latter is the more perfect knowledge.

There are also those who ask, not from natural impulse or from knowledge of the possibilities, but only to conform with the Divine Order in the Word: *Call upon Me and I will answer you.* Such a one is eminently a servant, *al-'abd,* for he asks without trace of self-interest, his concern being solely to conform with the order of his Master, *Rabb.* When asking is necessary, he asks to be a greater servant; if silence and renunciation are necessary, he is silent. When Job and others were severely tried, they did not request that their affliction be eased. Yet when their spiritual state necessitated asking, they were comforted. The immediacy or delay in granting what is requested depends entirely on the predestined measure appointed for it. If a request is made at just the predestined moment, the response is swift, but if its time is not yet due, either in this life or until the next life, the response will be postponed until that time. In either case, the principle of Divine Response is always "I am present." So consider well. As for gifts bestowed without any request, I meant an articulated request, for any Divine Action requires a request, whether expressed in words or simply inherent in the predisposition.

Similarly, praise of God is usually uttered, but in a spiritual sense praise is necessitated by the spiritual state, for the impulsion to praise God is the essential element that binds one to a Divine Name, expressing His activity or His transcendence. The servant is not aware of his predisposition, but only of the spiritual state, since knowledge of the predisposition is profoundly hidden. Those who receive God's gifts omit to make a request only because they know that God possesses predetermining knowledge. They have made themselves ever ready to receive whatever comes from Him and have divested themselves of their separative selves *(an-nafs)* and their aims.

There are those who know that God's knowledge of them in every state is commensurate with what they are in their state of pre-existent latency. They know that the Real bestows on them only what their latent essence *(al-'ayn)* expresses of Him. Amongst the Sufis none are higher or more intuitive than these, for they have realized the mystery of the Divine Predisposition. They in turn are divided in two groups: those who have this knowledge in general and those who have distinct knowledge, more elevated and complete. Such a person knows what God knows concerning himself, either because God reveals to him his Essence or because God has revealed this Essence in its infinite unfoldment of spiritual states. This is the higher gnosis, and its knower knows himself from the Divine Perspective, for his knowledge and God's are the same. But in respect to his ephemeral nature, his knowledge seems nothing but a Divine Benediction, one of a host of predetermined states in his Essence. This identity of knowledge is a Divine Benediction predetermined for the servant. In this regard the Word, *We will try you until we know,* bears an exact meaning utterly different from that imagined by those who have not drunk from the Source.

Returning to the subject of Divine Gifts, they come either from Essential Nature or from the Divine Names. Gifts of the first kind result from a divine Self-revelation, *tajalli,* that occurs only in a form of the essential predisposition of its recipient. The recipient sees nothing but his own form in the mirror of the Real. He cannot see the Real Itself, although he knows that he may see only his true form reflected in It. As in the case of a physical mirror, he does not see the mirror itself when looking upon the form in it, and he knows he beholds only his form. The analogy of a mirror is the closest and most faithful for a vision of divine Self-revelation.

Try, when you look at yourself in a mirror, to see the mirror itself, and you will find that you cannot do so. So much is this the case that certain people have concluded that the image perceived is interposed between the mirror and the eye of the beholder. This is the most they are capable of grasping. If you have experienced this spiritually, you have experienced all that is possible for a created being; do not seek or weary yourself attempting to reach beyond this, for there is nothing higher, nor is there beyond the point you have reached aught except the pure, undetermined, unmanifested Absolute. In your seeing your true Self, He is your mirror and you are His mirror in which He contemplates His Names, which are naught other than Himself.

Reality is prone to inversion and ambiguity. There are those amongst us who profess ignorance as part of their knowledge, saying with Abu Bakr that "To realize that one cannot know is to know." There are others who know, however, but who do not say such things, their knowledge eliciting silence rather than professions of ignorance. This is the highest knowledge of God, possessed only by the Seal of Messengers, *khatim ar-rasul,* and the Seal of Saints, *khatim al-awliya.** Thus none of the prophets and apostles can attain to it except from the Niche *(al-mishkat)* of the Seal of Messengers, nor are any of the saints able to attain it except from the Niche of the Seal of Saints, so that, in effect, none of the apostles can attain to it, when they do so, except from the Niche of the Seal of Saints.† This is because the offices of apostle and prophet — I mean one who brings the Sacred Law — are occasional, whilst sainthood never ceases.

It is not necessary for one who is perfect to be superior in everything and at every level, for spiritual men consider only precedence in the knowledge of God. They do not concern themselves with passing phenomena. Mark well what we have said. The Prophet likened the office of prophet to a wall of bricks, complete except for one brick, and He was the missing brick. However, where the Prophet sees the lack of one brick, the Seal of Saints perceives that two bricks are missing. The bricks of this wall are of silver and gold. The Seal of Saints is the two bricks, one silver and one gold, which complete the wall. Outwardly, he follows the Law of the Seal of Messengers, represented by the silver brick. This is his outer aspect, connected with the rules that he follows. Inwardly, however, he imbibes directly in Deity what he appears outwardly to follow, because he perceives the Divine Order as it truly is, represented by the golden brick. He derives his knowledge from the same source as the angel who unveils it to the Messenger. If you have understood my allusions, you have attained to the most efficacious knowledge.

Every prophet, from Adam until the last, assimilates what he has from the Seal of Prophets, even though he comes last in his temporal, physical manifestation, for in his spiritual reality he has always existed. Thus the Prophet said, "I was a prophet when Adam was between water and clay", whilst other prophets became

---

* *Khatim ar-rasul* is the title of Muhammad. It represents a cyclic function, whereas *khatim al-awliya* is secret and independent of time, being the archetype of spirituality. By degree of inspiration, every *rasul,* messenger, is *nabi,* prophet, but only those teaching a new sacred law are called *rasul.*

† *Al-mishkat,* the Niche of Light, is in Sufi thought the deepest centre in Universal Man.

such only when they awakened to their missions. In the same way, the Seal of Saints was a saint "when Adam was between water and clay", whilst other saints became saints only when they had gained all the necessary divine qualities, since these qualities of God are enshrined in the Names *al-wali*, the friend, and *al-hamid*, the adored. The Seal of Messengers, being also a saint, has the same relationship to the Seal of Saints as the other prophets and messengers have to him, for he is Saint, Messenger and Prophet, *al-wali, ar-rasul, an-nabi*.

As for gifts flowing from the Names of God, they are of two kinds: pure mercy, *rahmah*, such as a nourishing pleasure in the world that leaves no taint on the day of resurrection, which is bestowed by the Compassionate, *ar-rahman*; or a mixed mercy, such as a medicine disagreeable to the taste that brings relief. In his divine or qualified aspect, God always bestows gifts through the medium of one of the guardians of the Temple which consists of the Names. Sometimes God bestows a gift on His servant in His Name *ar-rahman*, the Compassionate, and this gift will be free of any admixture that is contrary to the servant's nature at that time, or of anything that works against him. Sometimes God gives in His Name *al-wasi'*, the Encompassing, so that the effect is universal, whilst at other times He gives through mediation of the Name *al-hakim*, the Wise, to serve only the best interests of the servant. He may give through the Name *al-wahhab*, the Bestower, giving as an unsolicited benediction, so that the recipient is under no obligation to render thanks or to perform works to merit the benediction. He may give through the Name *al-jabbar*, the Establisher of Order, in which case the cosmic environment and its necessities are considered. He may give in His Name *al-ghaffar*, the Forgiver, in which He considers the situation or state as it is at the time and gives moral protection. In this way are servants of the Divine spoken of as being immune and protected from sin. The giver is God as Keeper of the treasury of all possibilities which are dispensed according to a prescribed measure through the appropriate Name. Thus *He bestows on all He has created*, through the Name *al-'adl*, the Just, and similar attributes like *al-hakam*, the Arbitrator, *al-wali*, the Ruler, and *al-qahhar*, the Victorious.

The Divine Names of Deity are infinite because they are known by the infinite variety that derives from them. Nevertheless, they derive ultimately from a finite number of roots which are the matrices or abodes of the Names. Certainly, there is but one Reality, which embraces all these attributions and relations called the Divine Names. The Real grants that every name, infinitely manifest, should have its own reality by which to be distinguished from every other Name, and this distinguishing reality is the essence of the Name. In the same way, every Divine Gift is distinguished from every other by its own individual quality, even though all derive from a single source. The reason for this is the mutual distinction of the Names, there being no redundancy on the Plane of Divinity with its infinitude. This is a fundamental truth.

Such was the wisdom possessed by Seth, and it is his spirit that informs every other spirit expressing this kind of truth, save for the Spirit of the Seal, for his spiritual wisdom flows directly from Deity and not from any other spirit. Further, it is from his Spirit of the Seal that all other spirits receive their quintessence, even though they may be ignorant of the fact whilst in the physical body. They know it all essentially, whereas in the body they are ignorant of it. They at once know and do not know, taking on themselves the attribution of opposites, as does the Source Itself, as being at once the Majestic and the Beautiful, the Manifest and the Unmanifest, the First and the Last, this *coincidentia oppositorum* being his own essence. He knows and does not perceive, he contemplates and does not contemplate.

It is because of this knowledge that Seth is so named, his name meaning 'Gift of God'. In his hand is the key to the Divine Gifts in all their variety and their relations. God bestowed him on Adam, as his first unconditional gift, bestowing Seth as coming from Adam himself, since the son is the inner reality of the father, issuing from him and to him returning, and thus it is nothing alien to him. He whose understanding is divinely inspired will know this. In truth, every gift in the manifested universe follows this law. There is nothing received from God in anyone but what comes from his own self, however various the forms. Though this be the eternal truth of the matter, none knows it save certain of the initiated. Should you meet one who possesses such knowledge, you may have complete confidence in him, for he is a rare gem amongst the initiates of spiritual men.

Whenever a gnostic receives a spiritual intuition in which he contemplates a form that brings him new spiritual knowledge, the form he contemplates is none other than his own essential self. It is only from the tree of his own self that he will garner the fruits of his knowledge. In the same way, his image in a mirror is naught but himself, though the place or plane in which he sees his image produces inversions in the image in accordance with the intrinsic reality of that plane. In this way, something large appears small in a small mirror, long in a long mirror, and moving in a moving mirror. It may produce the inversion of this image from a particular plane, or it may produce an exactly corresponding reverse image, right reflecting right and left reflecting left. All this applies to the modes and properties of the mirroring plane on which the divine Self-revelation occurs.

Whosoever knows his predisposition knows what Divine Gifts he will receive, although not everyone who knows what he will receive also knows his predisposition until he has received, though he may sense it in a general way.

Certain thinkers of feeble intellect, having agreed that God does what He wills, go on to make assertions about God that contradict Divine Order. They go so far as to deny contingency, as also self-sufficient and relative essential being. The one who truly knows confirms contingency but knows its plane; he knows what is contingent and in what way it is so, even if it is in its essence necessary by virtue of something other than itself. Only those possessing knowledge of Deity understand this in detail.

It will be in the line of Seth that the last true Man will be manifested, bearing the Sethian Mysteries of Divine Wisdom, nor will any such be born after him. He will be the Seal of the Begotten. There will be born with him a sister who will be born first, so that his head will be at her feet. He will be born in China and will speak the language of that land. Sterility will then overcome the men and women of this land, and, although there will be much consorting, there will be no progeny. He will call them to the Divine without success, and when the Divine has absorbed him and those who believed, those remaining will live like beasts with no sense of right and wrong, given over to the law of the instinctual nature, devoid of intellect and Sacred Law. The Last Hour will overtake them.

THE WISDOM OF TRANSCENDENCE IN THE WORD OF NOAH

Al-Hikmat as-Subuhiyah

For those who truly know *ahl al-haqaiq*, the Divine Realities, affirmation of transcendence imposes conditionality and limitation on the Real, for he who asserts that Deity is purely transcendent is either ignorant or tactless. The exotericist who stresses only Divine Transcendence *(at-tanzih)* slanders and misrepresents the Real and all the messengers, albeit unwittingly.* He imagines that he has hit on the truth, whilst he has missed the mark, being like those who believe in part and deny in part.

It is known that the Scriptures express the Real as *shari'a*, traditional law, so that the generality of men grasp the apparent meaning. The élite, on the other hand, understand all the meanings hidden in that utterance, regardless of the terms in which it is expressed. The truth is that the Real is manifest in every created being and in every concept, even whilst He is hidden from all understanding, save for one who recognizes that the Cosmos is His form and Self, and who sees the world as the Divine Name, *az-zahir*, the Manifest. But He is also unmanifested Spirit, *al-batin*, the Unmanifest. In this sense He is, in relation to the manifested forms of the Cosmos, the Ruling Spirit.

Any logical definition of Man includes his inner and outer aspects, as is the case with anything that can be defined. As for the Real, He defines Himself by the sum of all possible definitions, for the forms of the Cosmos are limitless, nor can the definition of every form be known, except insofar as the forms are implicit in the definition of the Cosmos. Thus, a logical definition of the Real is impossible, for such a definition would require the ability to

---

* Islamic philosophy recognizes two ways of approaching the Divine: that of exaltation, separation or transcendence, *at-tanzih*, in which no attribute may be predicated of Deity; and that of comparison or analogy, *at-tashbih*, in which symbols manifest Divine Immanence. These complementary perspectives are intimately related to the *via negativa* and *via positiva* of European religious philosophy, and to the Hindu conceptions of *Nirguna Brahma* and *Saguna Brahma*.

define every form in the Cosmos, which is impossible. Therefore, a definition of the Real is impossible.

In the same way, one who draws comparisons with Deity without taking into consideration His incomparability restricts and limits Him and therefore does not know Him. He, however, who unites in his knowledge of Deity both transcendence and immanence in a universal way, even though it is not possible to know such a thing in detail because of the infinitude of cosmic forms, nevertheless knows Him in a general way, just as he may know himself generally but not in detail. Thus the Prophet said, "Who knows himself knows his Lord", linking together knowledge of God and knowledge of the self. In the Qur'an God says, *We will show them our signs on the horizons,* meaning the world outside you, *and in yourselves,* 'self' here meaning your inner essence, *until it becomes clear to them that All is the Real,* in that you are His form and He is your Spirit. You are in relation to Him as your physical form is to you. He is in relation to you as the governing spirit is to your physical form. This definition takes account of your outer and inner aspects, for the form that remains when the governing spirit is no longer present may no longer be called a man, but only a form having a human appearance, there being no real distinction between it and the form of wood or stone. The name 'man' may be given to such a form only figuratively by extension, but not properly.

On the other hand, the Real never withdraws from the forms of the Cosmos in any fundamental sense, so the Cosmos in its reality is necessarily implicit in the 'definition' of the divinity, *uluhiyah,* not merely figuratively as with a man when living in the body. Just as the outer form of Man gives praise with its tongue to its spirit and the soul that rules it, so also the cosmic forms glorify Him, although we cannot understand their praise because of our inability to comprehend all the forms of the Cosmos. All things are the 'tongues' of the Real, giving expression to the praise of the Real. Thus God says, *Praise belongs to God, Lord of the Universes,* for all praise refers to Him who both praises and is praised.

> If you affirm only His transcendence, you restrict Him,
> And if you affirm only His immanence, you limit Him.
> If you maintain both aspects, you are exempt from error,
> An Imam and a master in the spiritual sciences.

> Whoso would say He is two things is a polytheist,
> Whilst the one who isolates Him rationalizes Him.
> Beware of comparing Him if you envisage duality,
> And, if unity, beware of making Him separate.
> You are not He and yet you are He:
> You see Him in the essence of things both sovereign
>   and conditioned.

God says, *There is naught like unto Him*, asserting His transcendence, and He says, *He is the Hearing, the Seeing*, implying comparison. There are implicit in the first quotation comparison and duality, and in the second quotation transcendence and isolation.

Had Noah blended these two aspects in calling his people, they would have responded to his summons. He appealed to their outer and inner understanding, saying, *Ask your Lord to shield you, for He is forgiving*. Then he said, *I summoned them by night and by day, but my summons only made them more averse*. He states that his people turned a deaf ear to his summons only because they inwardly knew the proper way for them to respond to his summons. Those who know God understand the allusion Noah makes in respect to his people in that by blaming them he praises them, since he knows the reason for their not responding to his summons. His summons was made in a spirit of discrimination, even though whole truth is a conjunction, *al-qur'an*, and not a discrimination, *al-furqan*. *

One who is firmly rooted in knowledge of the conjunction does not dwell on the discrimination, for *al-qur'an* includes discrimination, but not vice versa. It is for this reason that the Qur'an, the union of the two aspects, was vouchsafed to Muhammad and the Community, which is the best granted to humanity. The quotation *There is none like unto Him* combines these two aspects. Had Noah uttered this kind of saying, his people would have responded to him, for he would have joined in the single verse the transcendent and immanent modes.

Noah summoned his people *by night*, in that he appealed to

---

* *Al-qur'an*, the Qur'an, literally means 'the recitation', but in Sufi symbolism it refers to immediate non-differentiated illumination, revelation as immediate knowledge. *Al-furqan*, discrimination, refers to revelation in general as *shari'a*, traditional law.

their intellects and spirits which are unseen, and *by day*, in that he appealed to their external senses. But he did not unite the two as in the verse *There is none like unto Him*. Thus their inner selves recoiled because of its discriminatory nature. In the verse *There is none like unto Him*, similarity is at once implied and denied. Because of this, Muhammad said that he had been granted knowledge of God integrating all His aspects. Muhammad did not summon his people *by night* and *by day*, but by night during the day and by day during the night.

Whosoever imagines that he sees the Real has no gnosis; he has knowledge who knows that it is his own essential Self he sees. Thus are people divided into those who know and those who do not know. What is required is the devotion of knowledge to contemplation, far removed from the fruits of ordinary thought. The heir of Muhammad recognizes that the summons to God is not a summons to His Essence, but to Him through the Divine Names. He says, *On the day when we will gather together the guarding ones in a band*, indicating that they will come before Deity in the Name of the Compassionate. We know that the Cosmos is under the rule of a Divine Name that protects everything in it.

In their deception they say, "Do not abandon your gods, neither Wadd, Suwa', Yaghuth nor Ya'uq, nor Nasr", for if they had renounced them they would have become ignorant of the Real. In every object of worship there is a reflection of the Real, whether it be recognized or not. In the case of Muhammad's heirs, He says, *Your Lord has decreed that you serve only Him*, meaning He has determined it. The one who knows recognizes Who is worshipped and in what form He is manifest to be worshipped. He also knows that distinction and multiplicity are merely like parts of a sensible form or the powers of a spiritual image. Indeed, in every object of worship God is worshipped.

The ignorant imagine objects to be endowed with divinity, and, were it not for this notion, neither the stone nor anything similar would be an object of worship. Thus He says, *Bid them name them*. If they had done so they would have called them stones, trees or stars. Had they been asked whom they worshipped, they would have said 'a god' and not 'God' or 'the God'. The man endowed with knowledge does not imagine in this way but knows that the object of worship is the vehicle of Divine Manifestation and worthy of reverence, but he does not restrict himself to the vehicle. The ignorant say, "We only worship them that they might bring us nearer to God." The man of knowledge says, *Your God is only One, so surrender yourselves to Him,* however He is manifest, *and bring glad tidings to those who conceal,* that is, who hide the fire of their nature though they call it 'a god' and not 'a nature'. He also says, *They have caused confusion to many,* meaning that they have perplexed them in the face of the multiplicity of the One in respect of His aspects and attributions. *In confusion,* that is, in spiritually self-effacing perplexity on the part of the heirs of Muhammad who said, "My Lord, increase my perplexity concerning You." He who experiences this perplexity is ceaselessly centered on the Pole, whilst he who follows the 'long' path is always turning aside from the Supreme Goal to search after that which is eternally within him, running after images as his goal. He has an imaginary starting-point and what he supposes to be a goal and what lies between them, whilst for the God-centered man there is no restriction of beginning or end, possessing as he does the most comprehensive existence and being the recipient of Divine Truths and realities.*

Because of their transgressions, transcending themselves so that they drowned in the seas of Divine Knowledge, which is what is meant by perplexity, *And they were cast into the fire,* which means the same as drowning. *When the seas swell,* where the same verbal root is used to denote the heating of an oven. *Nor will they find any helpers apart from God,* since their helpers are nothing

---

* In mystic Islam, the Pole refers to the symbolic North Pole, the equivalent to the East. The Divine Names arise in the East (which is why the three *magi* of Christian legend saw a star in the East even though they followed it *west*) but have their origin in the Pole. The North Pole is the location of the Midnight Sun, the highest Logos or Archangel which covers the Darkness of unknowable Deity, *deus absconditus.* The polar opposite of the Midnight Sun is the outer darkness of hell, utter alienation from the Divine. Thus the Pole represents the illumination of transcendental consciousness just as hell symbolizes the entrapment of the light of the soul. Our world is that in which the human being chooses his or her orientation, either to the east or west. By turning west, the soul risks endless imprisonment, whilst by turning east, the soul moves towards absorption in the dark iridescence of the Divine. This is why Ibn al-'Arabi says that the spiritually illuminated individual sees beyond beginnings and endings. The Sufi is 'perplexed' in that he recognizes at once the unknowability of Absolute Deity and the Divine Reflection in every form and expression.

other than God, and they are absorbed in Him forever. Thus, if He were to deliver them unto the shore of Nature, He would be lowering them from an eminent stage of spiritual attainment, even though all is God's, through God, indeed is God.

Noah said, "O my Lord!"; he did not say, "O my God", because the Lord is fixed, whereas the unqualified Divinity is manifold according to the variety of His Names and *every day He is engaged in some matter.* The Lord denotes an invariance of mode without which the appeal would not be appropriate. *Do not leave any of the deniers dwelling upon Earth,* beseeching that they be brought to the inner aspect of essential Unity. *If you spare them,* that is, leave them as they are, *they will confuse your servants,* meaning that they will perplex them and cause them to depart from their servanthood to the mysteries of lordship in themselves, and then they will consider themselves as Lords after being servants. They will indeed be servants who become as Lords. *My Lord, shield me,* that is, conceal me from my separate self and render my relative span and station unknowable in You since You are without measure. You say, *They do not assess God to the fullness of His measure. And my parents,* from whom I derived, namely, the Intellect and Nature. *And whosoever enters my house,* that is, into my heart, *believing,* that is, confirming the Divine Communication. *And the believers, both men,* meaning the intellects, *and women,* the souls.

And do not increase the oppressors, meaning those in darkness who belong to the Unseen, concealed behind dark veils, *except in destruction,* that is, in absorption into God. They have consciousness of themselves because their contemplation of the face of the Real absorbs them to the exclusion of their separative selves. Amongst the heirs is remembered the verse, *All perishes save His face,* the *destruction* in the above verse meaning this 'perishing'. Whosoever wishes to gain access to the mysteries of Noah must ascend to the Sphere of the Sun.

THE WISDOM OF HOLINESS IN THE WORD OF ENOCH

Al-Hikmat al-Quddusiyah

Elevation* may be ascribed in two ways, either with respect to position or to degree. An example of position is provided in His saying, *We raised him to a high position.* The most elevated position is that point round which the Spheres revolve, which is the Sphere of the Sun, where the spiritual form of Enoch (Idris) abides. There revolve round it seven higher Spheres and seven lower Spheres, numbering fifteen in all. The higher Spheres are those of Mars, Jupiter, Saturn, the Mansions, the Constellations, the Throne and the Seat. The lower Spheres are those of Venus, Mercury, the Moon, Ether, Air, Water and Earth. As being the pivot of the Spheres, Enoch is elevated as regards position. As for degree, it belongs to the heirs of Muhammad. God says, *You are the elevated ones and God is with you* in this elevation, since, although He is far above all position, He is not so in respect of degree.

When the soul in us, concerned with activity, fears the loss of attainment, He follows with His saying, *He will not nullify your deeds,* since action seeks position whilst knowledge seeks degree. Deity unites these two kinds of elevation for us, elevation of position through action and of degree through knowledge. Then He says, rejecting any suggestion of partnership, in His words, *God is with you. Exalt the name of your Lord, the Sublime,* that is, transcending any idea of partnership. The Universal Man is the most elevated of existing beings, but his elevation depends on an elevation of position or degree not derived from himself. He is elevated either because he occupies a high position in the Cosmic Order, or because he has a high degree, the elevation residing in

---

* The Arabic root from which 'holiness' derives is *qadasa*, 'to be far removed', which is associated with height or elevation. Holiness is the condition of being removed from unnecessary involvement in the world of effects, and is therefore an aspect of transcendence.

them and not in him. Regarding elevation of position, He says, *The Merciful is established on the Seat*, which is the supreme position. Alluding to elevation of degree, He says, *All perishes save His face*, and *All reverts to Him*, and *Can there be a god with God?*

When God says, *And We raised him to a high position*, He joins the adjective 'high' to the noun 'position', but His saying, *When your Lord said to the angels, "I am going to place on the earth a regent"*, refers to elevation of degree. He also says to the angels, *Are you displaying pride, or are you of the elevated ones?* associating elevation with the angels themselves. If this ascription were implicit in their being angels, all angels would share in it. But it is not a general ascription, and even though they are all defined as angels, we know that it refers to elevation of degree with Deity. Similarly, if the caliphs' elevation were implicit in their being men, all men would share in it. Since it is not general, we know that the elevation is one of degree.

The Elevated, *al-ali*, is one of the Divine Names, but above whom or what, since only He exists? More elevated than whom or what, since only He is and He is Elevated essentially in Himself? Everything is nothing but Him. In a certain sense, therefore, relative beings are elevated in themselves, since they are none other than He, and His elevation is absolute and not relative. This is because the essences, *al-a'yan*, are immutably unmanifest, *'adam*, beyond even the aroma of manifest existence, *al-wujud*, and they remain in that state in spite of the multiplicity of manifested forms. The Essence is Unique, *al-wahid*, amongst all and in all. Multiplicity exists only in the Divine Names, which are purely relationships and not manifest in themselves. Naught is except the Essence, which is Elevated in Itself, Its elevation being unrelated to any other. From this standpoint there is no relative elevation, although in respect of the aspects of existence there is differentiation. Relative elevation exists in the Unique Essence only insofar as It is manifest in many aspects. For this reason, it may be said that He is and is not He, and you are and are not you.

Abu Sa'id al-Kharraz, who is an aspect of the Real and one of His tongues, said, "God cannot be known except as uniting the opposites", in determining them through them. He is the First and the Last, the Manifest and the Unmanifest, the Essence of all that is manifest and all that remains hidden, even as He is manifesting

Himself. Thus, no one but He sees Him and He is hidden from no one, for He is manifest to Himself and hidden from Himself. None other than He bears the name Abu Sa'id al-Kharraz and all the other names given to ephemeral beings. The Unmanifest says "No" when the Manifest says "Me", and the Manifest says "No" when the Unmanifest says "Only I am." This is the nature of opposition, but there is only One who speaks and only One who listens, and they are One.

The Essence is Unique whilst the manifestations are various. This is well known, and every man knows this of himself, being the form of the Real. The realities are mingled, numbers subdividing the One. The One makes number possible, and number deploys the One. Enumeration is possible only because of the existence of that which is enumerated. The latter may exist or not exist, since something may be non-existent physically but exist intelligibly. Therefore there must be number and that which can be numbered, just as there must be the one to initiate the process by which it is itself developed. Each unit is a reality in itself, like nine or ten down to the lowest (two) or upward *ad infinitum,* although none of them are comprehensive, since each of them is a collection of units. Whosoever has understood what I have said about the numbers, namely, that to deny them is to affirm them, will know that the transcendent Reality is also the relative creature, even though the creature is distinct from the Creator. The Real is at once the created Creator and the creating creature. All this is One Essence, at once Unique *(al-'ayn)* and Many *(al-a'yan),* so consider what it is you see.

Isaac said, *O Father, do as you are commanded,* for the son is the essence of the father. Abraham saw only his own self to be sacrificed. *Then We ransomed him with a mighty sacrifice,* so that what previously appeared in human form then appeared as a ram, though it had appeared in the form of a son or, precisely, in a form which distinguishes father and son, since the son is the essence of the father. *He created from Adam's soul its mate,* so that Adam married his own soul. From him came forth both mate and child, for the Divine Order is One in multiplicity.

The same is true of Universal Nature, *at-tabi'ah,* and her multitudes of forms. Nature suffers no loss in displaying her forms nor any increase in assimilating them. What is manifest is She

Herself, though She is not the manifestation from the standpoint of formal distinction. One manifestation is cold and dry, another hot and dry. They are both one as regards dryness, but otherwise distinct. Universal Nature unites all of them. The natural order may thus be regarded as many forms reflected in a single mirror or as one form reflected in many mirrors. There is perplexity because of contrary perspectives. He who truly understands this is not confused, even when his knowledge passes from one state to another, for the change is due to shift in standpoint, which is one determinate view of the Real. The Real is diversified within the theatre of Self-revelation. He absorbs every perspective. He is determined only by His own Self-manifestation. There is naught but He.

> In one sense the Real is creature: so consider.
> In another He is not, so remember.
> One who understands my saying keeps perception
>   undimmed.
> Nor may one understand save he be endowed with
>   perception.
> Whether one asserts unity or division, the Self is Unique,
> And so are the Many that are and yet are not.

He who is Elevated in Himself enjoys *al-kamal,* the infinitude in which all realities and relationships are immersed, since none of the attributes can possibly apply to other than He. This includes all realities and relationships, whether they be moral or logical in the eyes of convention, reason or law. This applies only to the Real as Allah, the Name uniting all Names. As for the reality as other than God, manifested in some place or form, qualitative disparity occurs, either in location or hierarchical degree. If the form be the Universal Man, it embraces the essential perfection, since it is identical with the universal location in which it is manifest. The totality inherent in the Name Allah is implicit in that form, which is at once not He and not other than He.

Abu al-Qasim ibn Qissi alludes to this in his book *The Shedding of the Sandals,* where he says, "Every Divine Name is invested with all the Names." This is because every Name affirms the Essence as well as the specific aspect it enshrines. Therefore, implying the Essence, each Name partakes of all the Names.

Exemplifying the particular aspect of the Essence, each Name is distinct and unique. In this latter sense it is differentiated from every other Name, such as Lord, Creator, Fashioner and so on. In the former sense the Name is essentially the one Named, but other than He as representing some particular aspect.

If you have understood this treatise on elevation, you will see that it is elevation neither of position nor of degree. They are peculiar to persons in power, as sultans, governors, ministers, judges and holders of office, whether they are worthy or not. Self-sufficient elevation is not of this kind. It is quite possible for the wisest of men to be governed by the most ignorant who happens to hold a powerful office. The elevation of the latter is entirely relative to the office, whilst the former is elevated in himself. When the holder of office ceases to hold it, his elevation ceases also. This is not the case with a man of true knowledge.

THE WISDOM OF RAPTUROUS LOVE IN THE WORD OF ABRAHAM

Al-Hikmat al-Muhaymiyah

A braham was called the Intimate Friend of Allah, *khalil Allah*, because he had assimilated and penetrated all the attributes of the Divine Essence. The poet says,

> I have penetrated the course of the spirit within me,
> And thus was called Friend of the Divine.

In the same way, colour permeates what is coloured, so that the quality is confused with its substance, though not as a thing fills space. Abraham was so called because the Real permeated his form. Either affirmation is valid, since every determination points to an appropriate aspect beyond which it does not pass.

Do you not understand that the Real is manifest through the attributes of ephemeral beings, when He has informed us of that Himself, even through attributes of imperfection and blame? Do you not understand that the ephemeral being is manifest through the attributes of the Real, all of them being appropriate to it, from the first to the last, even as the attributes of ephemeral beings are appropriate to the Real? The words *Praise belongs to God* mean that all praise of the one who praises and the one who is praised returns to Deity. *To Deity all reality returns* includes all attributes whether praiseworthy or blameworthy, every attribute being one or the other. Whenever something suffuses another, it is assimilated into the other. The penetrating agent is disguised by that which is penetrated, so that the object is manifest, whilst the agent is unmanifest, the hidden reality. The latter nourishes the former, even as a piece of wool swells and expands because of the water that permeates it. If, to reverse the analogy, the Real is considered to be the Manifest and the ephemeral creature to be hidden within Him, the creature will assume all the Names of the Real, His hearing, His seeing, all divine modes and knowledge. If, however, the ephemeral creature is considered the manifest, and the Real the Unmanifest within him, then the Real is the power of hearing in the creature, as also in his sight, hand, foot and all his faculties. The Essence separated from all these relationships is not divinity, *ilah*. All these relationships originate in our eternally unmanifested essences, and we in our eternal potentiality make Deity a divinity by being that through which He knows Himself as Divine. Thus, He is not known as God until we are known.*

Muhammad said, "Who knows his true Self, knows his Lord", Man being the creature who knows Deity best. Certain sages, amongst them Abu Hamid al-Ghazali, taught that God can be known without reference to the created Cosmos, but this can be misleading. It is true that a primordial eternal essence can be known, but it cannot be known *as a divinity* without comparative knowledge, for it is the relative which confirms the Absolute, which is dependent on nothing. Spiritual intuition will further reveal that what is necessary to affirm divinity is other than the Real Itself, and that the Cosmos of ephemeral beings is nothing more than Its Self-revelation through eternally unmanifest essences of the forms which have no independent existence. A final spiritual intuition will show you that our forms manifest in Him, so that some of us are manifest to others in the Real, know each other and distinguish each other in Him. There are those of us who have spiritual knowledge of this mutual recognition in the Real, whilst others have not experienced the plane on which this occurs. I seek refuge in God, lest I be of the ignorant.†

As a result of these intuitions we see that we are judged only through ourselves; indeed, it is we who judge ourselves through ourselves, which is the meaning of the words *God's is the conclusive argument,* that is, against those veiled in ignorance who ask the Real why He has done this or that to them contrary to their

---

* Perhaps analogously, Krishna teaches in the *Bhagavad Gita* that the gods are nourished by *yajna*, sacrifices. *The Secret Doctrine* by H.P. Blavatsky refers to the "inane inactivity of pure Spirit". It is through incarnation in matter, the descent of *arupa* (formless) Spirit into limited realms of form, that Spirit awakens successively as consciousness, self-consciousness, and when totally free of delusive identification with forms, *svasamvedana*, pure self-analysing reflection. Without the process of limitation — the manifestation of the universe — the Unlimited cannot recognize Itself as It truly is.

† Mutual recognition in the Real is the mark of the Sufi adept. This is how all spiritual Teachers and mystics recognize one another instantly, regardless of seeming impediments of religious tradition, language or exoteric teachings.

interests. This is the truth revealed to the gnostics in the words *And He made their affair difficult for them.* They know that the Real has not done to them what is claimed, and they see that what was done to them came from themselves. His knowledge of them accords with what they are themselves. Divine Will is self-dependent as an essential attribute dependent on Divine Knowledge, which is in turn dependent on the object of Knowledge, which is you and your essential nature. Knowledge has no effect on the object of Knowledge, whilst what is known has an effect on Knowledge, bestowing on it of itself what it is.

Divine Discourse was formulated in accordance with the understanding of men and according to reason, which does not necessarily conform to what direct spiritual intuition reveals. Thus, although believers are many, gnostics endowed with spiritual intuition are few. *There are none of us but have a known station,* which is what you are in your eternal potentiality and in accordance with which you are manifest in existence, if, in truth, your reality includes the possibility of being manifested. If you say that existence may be attributed only to the Real and not to you, you will as eternal essence determine His existence. If you say that you have existence, you are nevertheless a determinant. For, even though the Real be the judge, *al-Hakam,* He only pours existence upon you, whilst you remain the judge and the judged. Therefore, praise only yourself and blame only yourself. Praise is due to the Real only as pouring forth existence.

You are the nourishment of the Real, for you bestow the contents of His Self-knowledge, whilst He is yours by bestowing existence. The Order is from Him to you — "Be!" You are called the one who is obligated, but He obligates you only in accordance with what your essential unmanifest reality bids Him.

> He praises me and I praise Him,
> He serves me and I serve Him.
> By my existence I affirm Him.
> As unmanifest essence I deny Him.
> He knows me, whilst I know Him naught,
> But I discover Him in contemplation.
> Where then is His Self-sufficiency,
> Since I help Him and grant Him glory?
> The Real has manifested me,

I lend Him knowledge and manifest Him,
Thus did the Divine Message come,
And its meaning is fulfilled in me.

It was because Abraham attained to this rank by which he was called the Friend of God that hospitality became a sacred act. Ibn Masarrah put him with Michael the Archangel, who is the source of provision. Food penetrates to the essence of the one fed, permeating every part. So also with divinity, though there are no parts but only Divine Stations, *maqamat*, or Names through which Divine Essence is manifest.

We are His as has been shown.
And we are our own as well.
He has no other becoming save mine,
We are His as we are through ourselves.
I have two aspects, He and me,
But He is not I in my I.
In me is His theatre of manifestation,
And we are for Him as vessels.

THE WISDOM OF REALITY
IN THE WORD OF ISAAC

Al-Hikmat al-Naqqiyah

The ransom of a prophet is a beast sacrificed as an offering,
But how can the bleating of a ram compare with the speech
  of Man?
How God the Mighty made mighty the ram for our sake or
  its sake, I know not.
No doubt the camel and the cow fetch a higher price,
But they are less than a ram sacrificed as an offering.
Would that I knew how a mere ram came to substitute for the
  Representative of the Compassionate.
Do you perceive a certain logic in the sacrifice,
The realization of gain and the lessening of loss?
No ephemeral being is higher than the mineral, and after it
  the plant,
From a certain standpoint and according to certain measures.
After the plant comes the animal, and all know their
  Creator by instinctual intuition and by clear signs.
As for the one called Adam, Man, he is bound by intelligence,
  thought and the garland of faith.
Concerning this said Sahl al-Tustari, a gnostic like ourselves,
Because we, one and all, are at the degree of spiritual vision,
Whosoever has contemplated what I have contemplated
Will say the same as I, in secret and in the open.
Do not consider contradicting words, nor sow seed in blind
  soil.
For they are the deaf, the dumb of whom the sinless one
  spoke in the verses of the Qur'an.*

---

* The poem reflects the root mystery in the connection between the human and the
Divine. Symbolically, the ram helps Man to be reconciled with Deity, and the animal is
sanctified by its participation in the sacrifice, for the animal is a symbolic substitute for
the ephemeral and terrestrial side of Man. The ram as Aries, the first sign of the zodiac, is
the brute energy which must be spiritualized and transmuted in a pilgrimage through the
signs that culminates in the Piscean dissolution through which the human being merges
with the Divine. Though man is superior to the animal by his participation in Intellect,
the animal kingdom is superior in its natural fidelity to the cosmic norm. In this sense,

Abraham, the Friend of the Divine, said to his son, *I saw in sleep that I was killing you for sacrifice.* The state of sleep is the plane of the Imagination, *hadarat al-khayal,* the plane of the Divine Presence in subtle forms. Abraham did not interpret his dream even though a ram appeared in the form of Abraham's son, because Abraham believed what he saw at face value. So his Lord rescued Isaac from Abraham's illusion *(al-wahm)* by the Great Sacrifice, which was the true expression of his vision, of which Abraham was unaware.* The formal Self-revelation of the Real on the plane of the Imagination requires a supplemental knowledge through which to discern what God intends by a particular form. Have you not considered what the Messenger of God conveyed to Abu Bakr concerning the interpretation of visions when he said, "I was right in some cases and mistaken in others"? When Abu Bakr asked him in which instances he had been right and in which wrong, he remained silent.

God said to Abraham, *O Abraham, you believed what you saw,* but He did not say, "You were right concerning what you saw", because he was faithful to his vision but took it at its face value, even though visions require interpretation. Thus, Joseph's master in Egypt says, *If you will interpret the vision.* Interpretation means to pass from the form of what one sees to the reality beyond it. Thus, in the dream Joseph interpreted, the cattle symbolized years of scarcity and plenitude. Had Abraham been true to the vision, he would have killed his son, for he believed that it was his son he saw, although from the divine point of view, it was nothing other than the Great Sacrifice in the form of his son. God saved Isaac from the mistaken notion that had entered Abraham's mind. In reality it was not a ransom from the divine standpoint, though the sacrifice of a ram was redemptive to Abraham. The senses formulated the sacrifice and the Imagination produced the form of Abraham's son. Had it been a ram he saw in the Imagination, he would have interpreted it as his son or as something else. Then

the lower kingdoms of Nature 'know' the Creator through instinctual intuition, *kashf,* and human beings sense ultimate Reality through spiritual vision, *al-ihsan.*

* Given what Ibn al-'Arabi has said previously, the child (Isaac) is Abraham's inmost individuated essence, his soul. Thus, the ram is a symbol for the soul, which must be sacrificed to Deity if total spiritual union is to occur.

God said, *This is indeed a clear test,* that is, a test of his spiritual knowledge, whether he knew the necessary interpretation in the perspective of the vision. Abraham knew quite well that the perspective of the Imagination requires interpretation, but was careless and did not deal with the perspective properly. Thus he believed the vision as he saw it.

Taqi ibn al-Mukhallad, the Imam and author of the *Musnad,* heard that the Messenger had said, "Whosoever sees me in sleep has seen me in waking, for Satan cannot take my form upon himself." Accordingly, Taqi ibn al-Mukhallad had a dream in which the Prophet gave him a bowl of milk to drink. He believed the vision literally and made himself vomit to prove its truth. Had he penetrated the meaning of his vision, the milk would have been recognized as wisdom, but instead he was denied as much knowledge as he had drunk in the form of milk. Remember that after the Prophet was brought a bowl of milk in a dream, he said, "I drank until I was satiated, and the rest I gave to 'Umar'." When asked, "What is your interpretation, O Messenger?" He said, "Knowledge", for he did not simply take the milk according to the form he saw, because he knew the perspective of vision and the necessity of interpretation.

It is well known that the bodily form of the Prophet perceived by the senses is buried in Medina, but the spiritual form and subtle essence have never been seen by anyone, as is true with every spirit. The spirit of the Prophet appears to one in the form of his body before he died, unaffected by decay. It is Muhammad appearing as spirit in a subtle form (*jasad*) resembling the buried body, for Satan is unable to assume this form.* Whosoever sees him in this mode accepts his commands, warnings and all he says, just as he would adopt his precepts in this world according to the explicit or implicit sense of the words. If, on the other hand, Muhammad gives him something in a dream, its form is a matter for interpretation. If, however, that thing proves the same in the sensory world as in the Imagination, the vision is one that does not require interpretation, and this is why Abraham, the Friend of

* Muhammad represents unwavering servitude, *'ubudiyah*, a spiritual quality which Satanic illusion cannot wholly imitate. The figure of Satan is for the Sufi what Mara is for the Buddhist.

Deity, and Taqi ibn al-Mukhallad dealt as they did with what they saw.

Since, then, the vision has these two aspects, straightforward and requiring interpretation, and since God has instructed us by what he did with Abraham (which teaching is connected to the Station of Prophecy), we know that of any vision we may have of the Real in a form unacceptable to the reason, we must interpret that form either from the standpoint of the conditioned divinity or the cosmic locus (al-makan) of the vision, or both. If, however, reason does not reject it, we can accept it as we see it, even as we shall look upon the Real on the other side.

> In every abode of being, the One and Only, the
> Compassionate, has forms, hidden and manifest.
> If you say, "This is the Real", you have spoken the
> truth, if "something other", you have interpreted.
> His manifestation applies in every abode equally,
> Indeed, He is ever unfolding His Reality in
> ephemeral becoming.
> When He manifests Himself to the sight, reason may rush
> to refute what is seen.
> He is accepted as manifested in the intellect and through
> the Imagination,
> But direct vision sees truly.

Abu Yazid al-Bistami said of this spiritual station, "If the Throne and all that surrounds it, multiplied a hundred million times, were to be in one of the many corners of the Heart of the gnostic, he would not be aware of it." Abu Yazid limited himself to the realm of corporeal forms. I say, however, that, even if limitless existence (if its limits could be imagined), together with the causative essence, were to be put into a corner of the Heart of the gnostic, he would have no consciousness of it. Though the Heart encompasses the Real and though it be filled, it nevertheless continues to thirst, as Abu Yazid has said. We have alluded to this spiritual station in these words:

> O You who create everything in Yourself, You enclose all
> You create.
> Though You create beings without limit within Yourself,
> You are both the Restricted, al-qabid, and the
> All-Encompassing, al-wasi'.

> Were all the creation of God in my heart, its resplendent
>   dawn would not shine there,
> Yet that which contains the Real can contain all creatures.
> How can this be, you who hear?

Every man creates by illusion *(al-wahm)* in the imaginative faculty that which has existence nowhere else, this being a facility common to all. The gnostic, however, by his spiritual will *(al-himmah)* creates that which has existence beyond the seat of this faculty, and indeed, the spiritual will maintains its existence without depleting itself in any way.* Should the attention of the gnostic be deflected from what he has created, it will cease to exist, except when the gnostic realizes all planes of existence. In that case deflection does not arise, for at all times he is present on some plane or another. When the gnostic who has such a realization creates something by his spiritual will, it is manifest in his form on every plane. In this case, the forms, each on its own plane, support one another, so that if the gnostic is absent on a certain plane or planes, whilst present on another or others, all the forms on all the planes are sustained by the form on the plane to which his attention is given. Lack of attention is never total, either with the generality of men or the initiate.

In saying this, I have unveiled a mystery that the initiates have always guarded from exposition, because it would seem to contradict the claim to be one with the Real. That is, the Real is never inattentive, whilst the servant is always inattentive to something or other. With respect to the maintenance of something he has created, the gnostic may say, "I am the Real", but his maintenance of that thing cannot be compared to the maintenance

---

* The Imagination, *al-khayal*, is common to all human beings in its passive mode. When it is aroused by the spiritual will, it creates lasting forms. Spiritual will, *al-himmah*, encompasses the ideas of the force of spiritual decision, of concentration and of aspiration towards the Real, hence the creative power of Truth. *Al-himmah* is set opposite *al-wahm*, illusion, conjecture or opinion. For Ibn al-'Arabi, imagination with spiritual will is creative Imagination, and imagination without it is fancy and fantasy. There are analogies with the soul's active and passive mirroring of the One in the philosophy of Plotinus, and with the reflection of *Kriyasakti* and *Itchasakti* in the human constitution as taught in Hindu thought. When spiritual will is present, according to Ibn al-'Arabi, Imagination is a ray of Divine Activity.

exercised by the Real.* To the extent that he is inattentive to some form on its plane, he is a servant as distinct from the Real. This whole question, I have been told, has never previously been committed to writing, either by me or any other, until now. It is unique and without precedent. Take care lest you forget, for that plane in which you remain present with the form may be compared to the Book of which God said, *We have missed nothing in the Book,* for it comprises all that has come to pass and all that has not come to pass. Only he will truly know what we have said whose essential Self is a united totality, *al-qur'an.* For one who fears God, *He will make a discrimination for him,* and he is as we have mentioned in discussing the distinction between servant and Lord. This discrimination *(al-furqan)* is the loftiest that one can conceive.

> At one time the servant is a Lord, without a doubt,
> At another time the servant is a servant, most certainly.
> If servant, he encompasses the Real,
> If Lord, he is in a conditioned life.
> As servant he perceives the essential Self
> And hopes range widely from him.
> As Lord he sees all existence, from earth to angel, all
>   making demands of him.
> In himself he is quite unable to answer their demands,
> And for this reason you may see gnostics weeping.
> So be the servant of a Lord, not Lord of a servant,
> Lest you become prey to the fire of fusion.

---

* The great Sufi mystic al-Hallaj was executed for saying "I am the Real", a horrendous blasphemy to orthodox ears. He was only affirming, though perhaps too publicly, that which all Sufi initiates know, union with the Divine. Yet fellow Sufis found his death ironically appropriate, for if he had achieved the absolute union which would make his claim true, he would no longer exist to speak, for he would have been wholly absorbed in the Real. Ibn al-'Arabi is speaking of that union which allows a residuum of individuality. This is reminiscent of the Buddhist distinction between *nirvana* 'with remains' and *nirvana* 'without remains'.

THE WISDOM OF LIGHT
IN THE WORD OF JOSEPH
Al-Hikmat an-Nuriyah

T he light of this luminous Wisdom extends over the plane
of the Imaginative Presence, which is the first principle
of inspiration, *al-wahi*, according to the people of
Providence.* 'Aishah, the wife of the Messenger, said, "Revelation
began with the Messenger of God as the true dream, which was as
clear as the breaking of dawn whenever he saw it, and nothing in it
was obscure." 'Aishah's knowledge was limited to this. She added
that he had been in this state for six months, after which the
angel Gabriel came to him. What she did not know was that the
Messenger had said, "Men sleep and when they die they awaken."
All that is seen in sleep is of a similar nature, though the conditions
are different. She spoke of six months, whereas in reality his
whole earthly life was like this, a dream within a dream. All things
of this kind constitute the realm of the Imagination, *'alem al-khayal*,
and because of this they are interpreted. That is, the reality which
assumes a certain form appears under another form, so that the
interpreter proceeds from the form seen by the dreamer to the
form of the reality in itself, if he is successful, as, for example, the
appearance of knowledge in the form of milk. The Messenger
proceeded in his interpretation from the form of milk to the form
of knowledge, transposing from one plane to another.†

---

* The Divine Presence is directly experienced in rapturous contemplation and ecstatic
meditation, and it is discovered in five modes, corresponding to the highest states of
consciousness. *Hadarat al-ghayb al-mutlaq* is the Divine Presence in the Absolute and
Unknowable. *Hadarat al-ghayb al-mudafi* is the Divine Presence in the Unmanifest, and
Hadarat ash-shahadat al-mutlaqah is the Divine Presence in the Manifest. *Al-hadarat
al-jam 'iyah* is the Divine Presence in its impartite integrity. The Imaginative Presence
referred to here is *hadarat al-khayal*, the Divine Presence in the realm of Imagination.

† The Sufi mystic recognizes the necessity of interpretation of dreams and visions
through a transposition of forms which is neither arbitrary nor mechanical. "The world
is Imagination", *al-kawmu khayal*, means that the universe is illusory in comparison with
the Real, and also that the Cosmos is constituted of reflections of eternal and archetypal
realities. Thus the world of Imagination, *'alem al-khayal*, is also the world of analogies,

When the Prophet used to receive a Divine Inspiration, he was withdrawn from all usual sensations, covered with a cloak and absent from everyone present. When the inspiration ceased, he returned to this world. He perceived only on the plane of the Imagination, even though he was not sleeping. In the same way, the appearance of the Angel to him as a man was also from the plane of the Imagination, since Gabriel is not a man, but rather an angel who assumed human form. This form was transposed by the gnostic beholder to its own true form. He said, "It is Gabriel who has come to teach you your religion"; but he also said, "Return the man's greeting", calling him a man because of the form in which he had appeared. Then he said, "This is Gabriel", acknowledging the original form of the imaginary human form. He was right from the viewpoint of the physical eye and also right in that it was, without doubt, Gabriel.

Joseph said, *I saw eleven stars and the sun and moon prostrating before me.* He saw his brothers in the form of stars and saw his father and stepmother as the sun and the moon. This is Joseph's viewpoint. However, had it been so from the standpoint of those appearing as stars, their manifestation would have been according to their wishes. Since they had no knowledge of what Joseph saw, his perception occurred through his own imaginative faculty. When Joseph told Jacob of his vision, Jacob understood the situation and said, *My son, do not relate your vision to your brothers, lest they conspire against you.* Then he absolved his sons of conspiracy and transposed it to Satan, who is the very essence of deceit, saying, *In truth, Satan is Man's certain foe,* which is true exoterically. Later on, Joseph said, *This is the original meaning of my vision, which my Lord has made true,* that is, he has manifested it tangibly, whereas it had been in a form from the Imagination. Concerning this, Muhammad said, "Men sleep", whilst Joseph said,

---

'alem al-mithal. Imagination is not limited to the subjective experience of the individual, for affirming that "the world is Imagination" implies the cosmic function of imagination. In meditation, the individual's faculty of imagination is gradually awakened and merges with Cosmic Imagination, transcended only by pure spiritual Intellect, the active intuition which perceives realities directly. The universe as macrocosmic Imagination rather than ultimate reality is suggested by Patanjali in the *Yoga Sutras* (II, 21) when he says, "For the sake of the Soul alone, the Universe exists." To one of fully awakened Intellect, the universe is an illusion.

My Lord has made it true, but he was in the position of one who dreams that he has risen from a dream and interprets it. Such a one does not know that he remains asleep and dreaming, but when he does wake, he says, "I saw such and such, which, dreaming that I had waked, I interpreted." Joseph's situation is analogous to this. Note the difference between the perceptions of Muhammad and of Joseph when he said, *This is the real meaning of my vision, which my Lord has made true,* by which he means sensible. It could not be otherwise, since the Imagination operates only in the sensible.

Know that what is other than the Real, that is, the Cosmos, is, in relation to the Real, as a shadow is to that which casts the shadow. It is the shadow of Deity and is the same as the relation between Being and the Cosmos, since the shadow is doubtless something sensible. It is that on which the shadow is cast, since if it were possible that it should cease to be, the shadow would be intelligible and not sensible, and it would exist potentially in the very thing that cast the shadow. That on which the Divine Shadow — the Cosmos — appears is the eternal essences, *al-a'yan,* of possibilities, *mumkinat.* The shadow is projected on them, and the shadow is known to the extent that the Being of the pristine Essence is located upon it. It is by the Divine Name, *an-nur,* the Light, that the shadow is perceived. This shadow extends over the essences of possibilities in the form of the unknown Mystery. Have you not observed that shadows tend to darkness, indicating their imperceptible character by reason of the remote correspondence between them and their origins? The source of the shadow is white, but the shadow itself is black.*

You observe that mountains appear to be black in the distance, though they are in themselves some other colour. The cause of the dark appearance is only the distance. The same holds true of the blueness of the sky, which is also the effect of distance on the senses with respect to non-luminous bodies. In the same way, the essences of possibilities are not luminous, being non-existent, yet potential. They cannot be described as existing because existence is light. Even luminous bodies are rendered small by distance. Such

* According to Ibn al-'Arabi, the Light, *an-nur,* arises from imperceptible Darkness and gives rise to perceptible darkness. In Sufi cosmology, blue approaches black and is the colour of impenetrable depths.

bodies are perceived as small, even though in themselves they are large. For example, evidence suggests that the sun is 166.375 times the size of the earth, whilst to the eye it is no larger than a shield. This, too, is the effect of distance.* No more is known of the Cosmos than is known from a shadow, and no more is known of the Real than one knows of the origin of a shadow. Insofar as he has a shadow, he is known, but insofar as the form of the one casting the shadow is not perceived in the shadow, the Real is not known. For this reason we say that the Real is known to us in one sense and unknown in another.

Have you not seen how your Lord extends the shade; if He so willed He would make it stay, meaning, it would be in Him potentially, which is to say that the Real is not revealed to ephemeral beings before He manifests His shadow, the shadow being like those beings not yet manifested in existence. *Then We made the sun as an indication of it,* which is His Name, *an-nur,* the Light, of which we have spoken and by which the senses perceive. Shadows have no existence without light. *Then We take it back to Ourselves easily,* because it is His shadow, since from Him it is manifest and to Him the whole manifestation returns: the shadow is none other than He. Everything we perceive is nothing but the being of the Real in the essences of ephemeral beings. With reference to the Supreme Self, *al-huwiyah,* of the Real, it is Its Being, whereas, with reference to the variety of its forms, it is the essences of ephemeral beings. Just as it is always called a shadow because of the variety of forms, it is always called the Cosmos and "other than the Real". In its unity as the shadow, it is the Real, being the One, *al-ahad,* the Unique, *al-wahid,* but in the multiplicity of its forms it is the Cosmos. Therefore, understand and realize what I have explained to you.

If what I say is true, the Cosmos is illusory, *mutawahham,* without any real existence, and this is what one means by the Imagination. That is to say, you imagine that the Cosmos is something separate and autonomous, outside the Real, when in truth it is not. Have you not observed that shadows are connected to the one who casts them, and would not its becoming separated

---

* The current astronomical estimate is that the sun is roughly 1,300,000 times the size of the earth, reinforcing Ibn al-'Arabi's point.

be absurd, since nothing can be separated from its own essence, *adh-dhat?* Therefore, know your own self, who you are, what is your identity and what your relationship with the Real. Consider well in what way you are real and in what way you are part of the Cosmos, yet separate, other and so on. In this respect sages are superior to one another.

The Real is, in relation to a particular shadow, small or large, more or less pure, as light in relation to the glass that separates it from the beholder, for whom the light has the colour of the glass even though the light itself is colourless. This is the relationship between what one sees and the Divine Light, and between your reality and your Lord. If you were to say the light is green (because of the green glass), you would be right in terms of your senses, and if you were to say that it is not green, but in fact it is colourless by deduction, you would be right in terms of sound intellectual reasoning. That which is seen may be said to be a light projected from a shadow, which is the glass, or a luminous shadow, according to its degree of purity.* Thus, the Real manifests the form of the Real to a greater extent in him who has realized himself than in him who has not. There are those of us in whom the Real has become their hearing, sight and all their faculties and limbs, according to signs given us in the Divine Message transmitted by the Prophet. Nevertheless, the shadow exists essentially, for the pronoun 'his hearing' refers to him as shadow. Other servants are not of this attainment, which is more closely attached to the being of the Real than others.

If things are as we have said, know that you are Imagination, and all that you perceive as other than yourself is also Imagination. Relative existence is imagination within imagination, the only Reality being Deity as Self and Essence, independent of His Names. The Divine Names have a double significance. One connotation is God Himself who is what is named, and the other is that by which one Name is distinguished from another. Thus, the

---

* Perception through the senses corresponds to the level of understanding mediated by analogy, *al-tashbih*, which is always symbolic. Reasoning with the mind corresponds to transcendental understanding, *al-tanzih*, which involves withdrawal from the senses. The subjective creation of images is imagination subject to ignorance, whereas Cosmic Imagination is an active power based on spiritual knowledge. The Cosmos is an illusion when compared to the incomparable Unknowable.

Forgiving, *al-ghafur*, is not the Manifest, *az-zahir*, or the Unmanifest, *al-batin*, nor is the First, *al-awwal*, the Last, *al-akhir*. You already know that each Name is essentially every other Name and that it is not any other Name. In the first sense, being essentially the other, the name is the Real, whilst in the second sense, being not the other, it is the imagined Reality. Exalted is He who Alone is evidence of Himself Alone, and who is Self-subsisting. There is nothing in Being outside of that which is implicit in the Divine Unity, and there is naught in the Imagination but what is implicit in cosmic multiplicity. Grasping multiplicity, one is caught up in the Cosmos, the Divine Names as distinct appellations, and the Cosmic Names. Discerning the Unity, one is with the Real in His Essence as Self-sufficient beyond all worlds. Being transcendentally Self-sufficient, He is independent of and beyond all nominal relationships, since the Names, whilst implying Him as the Essence, also imply the realities named, whose effects they manifest.

Say: He God is One, in His Unique Self; *God the Eternal Refuge*, in respect of our dependence on Him. *He begets not*, in His Identity or in relation to us. *Nor is He begotten* and *He has no equal?* have the same significance. Thus, He depicts Himself and isolates His Essence in the words *God is One*, though the multiplicity appearing through His Attributes is well known. We beget and are begotten, depend on Him and compete one with another. However, the Unique One transcends all these attributes, having no need of them or of us. God's Unity, in regard to the Divine Names necessary to our existence, is a unity of multiplicity, though in regard to His complete independence from the Names and therefore from us, it is unity of Essence, for both of which the Name *al-ahad*, the One, is used.

God manifested shadows lying to the right and the left as clues for you in knowing yourself and Him, that you might know who you are, your relationship with Him and His with you, and so that you might understand how or according to which Divine Truth all that is other than God is depicted as being completely dependent on Him and as being mutually interdependent. In addition, you know how and by what truth God is depicted as utterly independent of men and all worlds, and how the Cosmos is depicted as both mutually independent with respect to its parts and mutually dependent. Without doubt, the Cosmos is fundamentally dependent on causes, the greatest of which enjoys the causality of the Real. The Divine Causality on which the Cosmos depends is the Divine Names. Besides this, it is well known that we are also mutually dependent. Our true names are God's Names, since all depends on Him. At the same time, our essential Selves are His shadow. He is at once our identity and not our identity. Here we have just paved the way for you.

THE WISDOM OF THE HEART IN THE WORD OF SHU'AIB

Al-Hikmat al-Qalbiyah

Know that the Heart, that is, the Heart of the gnostic, derives from Divine Compassion, though embracing more than it, since the Heart encompasses the Real and Compassion does not. This is alluded to and supported in tradition. The Real is the subject rather than the object of Compassion, and it has no defining power with respect to the Real. Specifically, one might say that God has described Himself as the Breath, *nafas*, from *tanfis*, meaning to cause rest or relief. It is also true that the Divine Names are in one sense the thing named, which is none other than He. Yet they require the very realities they bestow, which constitute the Cosmos. For divinity *(uluhiyah)* implies and requires that which depends on it, just as lordship requires servanthood. Neither would have any existence or meaning without the other. Whereas the Real in essence is beyond all need of the Cosmos, lordship does not enjoy such a position. In truth, the difference is between the mutual dependency implicit in lordship and the Self-sufficiency of the Essence. Indeed, the Lord is, in its reality and qualification, none other than this Essence. When, however, differentiation and opposition arise by virtue of the variety of relationships, the Real depicts Itself as the bestower of compassion on His servants. The Real first expressed the Breath, called the Breath of the Compassionate, from lordship by creating the Cosmos, which lordship and all the Names require by their very nature. Clearly Compassion embraces all things, including the Real, being more or less as encompassing as the Heart in this respect.

Know that the Real, confirmed by tradition, in His Self-manifestation transmutes Himself in the forms. Know also that when the Heart embraces the Real, it embraces none other than He, since it is as if the Real fills the Heart. When the Heart contemplates the Real in Its Self-manifestation to it, it is incapable of contemplating anything else whatsoever. Abu Yazid al-Bistami has said of the Heart of the gnostic that "Were the Throne and all it comprises to be placed one hundred million times in the corner of the gnostic's Heart, he would not be aware of it." On this question Abu-L-Qasim al-Junayd said, "When the contingent is linked with the Eternal, there is nothing left of it." When the heart embraces the Eternal One, how can it possibly be aware of anything contingent and created? Since the Self-manifestation of the Real varies according to the variety of forms, the Heart is necessarily wide or restricted according to the form in which God manifests Himself. The heart can comprise no more than the form in which the Self-manifestation occurs. The Heart of the gnostic or the Perfect Man is like the setting of the stone in a ring, conforming to it in every way, being circular, square, or any shape of the stone itself, for the setting conforms to the stone and not otherwise.* Some oppose this view by saying that the Real manifests Himself in accordance with the predisposition of the servant. But this is not true, since the servant is manifest to the Real according to the form in which the Real manifests Himself to him. God manifests Himself in two ways: unseen manifestation and sensible appearance. It is from the unseen that the predisposition of the Heart is bestowed, being the essential Self-manifestation, the very nature of which is to be unseen. This is the Divine Identity in accordance with which He calls Himself *He*. This Identity is His alone in all and from all eternity.

None other than God bestows on the Heart its predisposition in accordance with His saying, *He bestows upon everything He has created*. Then He lifts the veil between Himself and the servant, and the servant sees Him in the form of his belief. Indeed, He is the content of the belief. Neither the Heart nor the eye of the Heart sees anything but the form of its belief concerning the Real. It is the Reality contained in the belief whose form the Heart encompasses. It is this Reality that manifests itself to the Heart, so that the Heart recognizes it. Thus the eye sees only the Reality believed in, and there are a great many beliefs. He who restricts the Real to his own belief denies Him when manifested in other

---

* The title of this work, *The Seals of Wisdom, Fusus al-Hikam*, derives from this analogy. According to Ibn al-'Arabi, each prophet, messenger or teacher is the setting for one jewel of Divine Wisdom.

beliefs, affirming Him only when He is manifest in his own belief. He who does not restrict Him thus does not deny Him but affirms His Reality in every formal transformation, worshipping Him in His infinite forms, since there is no limit to the forms in which He manifests Himself. The same is the case with the gnosis of God, and there is no limit for the gnostic in this respect. The gnostic ever seeks more knowledge of Him, saying, *O Lord, increase me in knowledge.* Thus possibilities are without end on both sides, that of the Absolute and that of relative being.

When you consider His saying, "I am his foot with which he walks, his hand with which he strikes, and his tongue with which he speaks", why do you make a distinction by saying it is all the Real, or it is all created? It is all created in a certain sense, but it is also the Real in another sense, the Essence being One. In essence, the form of a Self-manifestation and the form of the one who perceives it are the same, for He is both the Self-manifestation and the form of the one subject and the object of that manifestation. Consider then how wonderful is Deity in His Identity and in His relation to the Cosmos through the realities inherent in His Beautiful Names.

> Who is here and what is there?
> Who is here is what is there.
> Who is universal is particular,
> And Who is particular is universal.
> There is one Essence only,
> The light of the Essence is also darkness.
> One who heeds these words will not
> Fall into confusion.
> In truth, only he knows what we say
> Who is possessed of spiritual power.

Surely in that is a reminder for him who has a heart, by reason of His ceaseless transformation through all the varieties of forms and attributes. Nor does He add, "for him who has an intellect". This is because the intellect restricts and seeks to define the truth within discursive qualifications, whilst in fact the Real does not admit of limitation. This is not just a reminder to the intellectuals and purveyors of doctrinal formulations who contradict one another and denounce each other — *and they have no helpers.*

The god of one believer has no validity before the god of one who believes something else. Though a supporter of a particular belief defends what he believes and champions it, that in which he believes does not support him, and so he has no effect on his opponent's belief. Thus, also, his opponent derives no assistance from the god formulated in his own belief — *they have no helpers.* This is because the Real has denied to the gods of creeds and formulations any possibility of rendering assistance, since each one is restricted to itself. Both the one assisted and the one who assists are the Totality, *majmu'*, of the Divine Names. For the gnostic the Real is known and never denied. Those who know in this world will know hereafter. For this reason He says, *for one who is possessed of a heart,* that is, one who understands the formal transformations of the Real by adapting himself formally, so that from himself he knows the Self. Thus his self does not differ from the Divine Identity Itself. No being, now or in the future, is other than His Identity. He is the Identity Itself.

God is the one who knows, who understands and who affirms in some particular form, just as He is also the ignorant one, the uncomprehending, the unknown in another form. This, then, is the lot of one who knows the Real through His Self-manifestation and witnesses Him in the totality of formal possibilities. This is what is meant by the saying, *for one possessed of a heart,* that is, one who turns *(taqlib)* towards the Real in all the diversity of the forms.* People of faith follow blindly the utterances of prophets and messengers concerning the Real, but not those who slavishly follow thinkers who derive their knowledge from intellectual processes. People of faith are indicated in His saying, *or gives ear* to what God has said through the lips of the prophets. By this is meant one who gives ear in witness on the plane of the Imagination and its use, suggested in the saying of the Prophet, "that you should worship God as if you saw Him", for *God is in the* qiblah *of the one who prays.* Thus he is a witness. It cannot be said of one who follows the mere thinker and is bound by his thoughts that he is one who gives ear, since one who gives ear is also a witness to what we have mentioned. Therefore, O Friend, realize

---

* Turning, *taqlib*, towards the Real is implied in the concept 'in the Heart', *al-qalb*. The devout turns in the appropriate direction, *qiblah*, towards Mecca to pray.

the truth of this Wisdom of the Heart that I have set forth for you.

This Wisdom has a special connection with Shu'aib because of its innumerable ramifications, *tasha'ub*, for each and every creed is a particular path. Thus, when the covering of this earthly life is drawn back, each one will see either what is disclosed according to his belief or what is contrary to it. He says, *And there is manifest to them of God what they had not expected to see.* Take for example the Mu'tazilite, who believes that God will carry out His threat to punish the sinner who dies unrepentant. When he dies and experiences Divine Compassion, since providence has already decreed that he should not be punished, the Mu'tazilite finds that God is Forgiving and Compassionate. There is manifest to him that which he had not considered in his belief.* In respect to God in His Identity, certain of His servants have judged in their belief that God is this or that, and when the covering is removed, they see the form of their belief, since it is true, and they believe in it. When, however, the knot of belief is loosened, belief ceases to bind his heart and one knows by intuitive contemplation. After his sight has been sharpened, myopia will not recur. Some servants have God disclosed to them in various forms, differing from those first seen, since a particular Self-manifestation is never repeated. He then holds this to be true with respect to His Identity, so that *there is manifest to them of God*, in His Identity, *what they had not considered*, before the drawing back of the veil.

We have discussed progress in the Divine Sciences in our *Book of Theophanies*, where we talk of those belonging to the mystic Order that we have encountered in vision, *kashf*, and what we taught them on this question. Amazingly, such a one is always advancing even though he is not aware of it, because of the subtlety and fineness of the veil and the ambiguity of forms. He says, *It is brought to them in an ambiguous way.* This veil is not the same as the other one, for similars in the sight of the gnostic, though similars, are also different from each other. That is because he who has attained to realization sees multiplicity in the One, just

---

* The Mu'tazilites taught that God acts in a supremely rational way and concluded that the human mind, being rational, can predict Divine Action. Ibn al-'Arabi recognizes through mystic insight that the effects of Divine Activity are too complex and numinous to be understood by such a simplistic view.

as he knows that essential Oneness is implicit in the Divine Names, even though their individual realities are various and multiple. It is a multiplicity intelligible in the One in His Essence. In manifestation it is a discernible multiplicity in a single essence, just as the Primal Substance is assumed in the case of every form, which springs in reality from a single substance. He, therefore, who knows himself in this way knows his Lord, for He created him in His image; indeed, He is his very identity and reality. It is because of this that none of the scholars have attained to knowledge of the Self and its reality except those theosophists amongst the messengers and the Sufis. He who seeks to know by theoretical speculation is flogging a dead horse. Such are certainly those *whose endeavour is awry in this world, but who consider that they do well.* He who seeks to know this matter other than by its proper course will never grasp its truth.

THE WISDOM OF DESTINY IN THE WORD OF EZRA

Al-Hikmat al-Qadariyah

Know that the Decree *(qada')* is God's determination of things, which is limited to what He knows of them in them. His knowledge of things depends on what the knowable reveals from what they are eternally in themselves essentially. Destiny *(qadar)* is the precise timing of the manifestation and dissolution of things in their essence. This is the mystery of Destiny itself *for him who has a heart, who hearkens and bears witness, for God has the last word*; for the Determiner, in actualizing His determination, complies with the essence of the object. The thing determined, in strict accordance with its essential state, itself determines the activity of the Determiner, since every governor is itself governed by that which it governs or determines. Therefore, Destiny is unknown only because of the immediacy of its manifestation. Though greatly sought after and zealously pursued, it is seldom recognized.

The Messengers, as messengers rather than as saints or gnostics, conform to the spiritual level of their communities. The knowledge with which they have been imbued fits the needs of their communities precisely, since communities vary in need. He says, *We have given some of these apostles more than others.* Just as the doctrines and regulations deriving from their essences are various according to their predispositions, so He says, *We have favoured some of the prophets over others. God has favoured some of you over others in the matter of provisions.* Provisions may be either spiritual, like learning, or sensible, like food, and the Real manifests it according to a known measure to which a creature is entitled, since *God has given to everything He has created* and *He sends down as He wills.* He wills in terms of what He knows and by what He determines. Thus the timing of Destiny ultimately belongs to that which is known, whilst the Decree and knowledge as well as will and wish, *al-mashi'ah* and *al-iradah*, depend on Destiny.

The mystery of Destiny is amongst the most glorious kinds of knowledge, for insight into it is granted only to one who has been selected for perfect gnosis. Knowledge of this mystery brings unflawed repose and terrible torment, for it combines the opposites by which God is described as wrathful and approving, *al-muntaqim* and *al-'afuw*. The Divine Names polarize in this mystery. Its truth holds sway over both the Absolute and the relative, for nothing is more perfect, powerful and mighty through the totality of its dominion, both direct and indirect. Each of the prophets derives his knowledge from one kind of Divine Revelation, and so the Heart of each is simple from the intellectual point of view. The prophets know the limitations of the discursive intellect when it comes to the understanding of things essentially. Verbal communication is also limited in conveying what is accessible only to direct experience. Perfect knowledge is gained only through a divine Self-revelation or when God draws back the veils from Hearts and eyes so that they might perceive things, eternal and ephemeral, non-existent and existent, impossible, necessary or permissible, as they are in their eternal reality and in essence.

Ezra sought a special way and received the rebuke related to him. Had he sought the Divine Inspiration we have discussed, he would not have been rebuked. His simplicity of heart is shown in his saying (in another connection), *How can God revive Jerusalem after its oblivion?* His character is summed up in this saying even as Abraham's character is summed up in his saying, *Show me how you revive the dead.* Such a request demanded an active response, which the Real accordingly made evident in him when He said, *God caused him to die for a hundred years and then brought him forth alive.* He said to him, *Behold the bones, how We have joined them together and then clothed them in flesh.* In this way, he perceived directly and with immediate perception how bodies grow forth. But he had asked about Destiny, which is known only through a revelation of things in their latent state of non-existence. This was denied him, for such knowledge is the prerogative of Divine Awareness. None other than He knows such things, since it concerns the primordial keys, the keys of the Unseen. Nevertheless, God can inform those of His servants whom He wishes about some of these things. They are called keys because they signify a state of opening, which is the process of bringing into manifestation or, if you prefer, the state in which the capacity to exist becomes part of what is destined to exist, a state which only Deity can be said to experience. That is because the keys of the Unseen are never manifested or unveiled, since all capability and activity belong to one who has Absolute Being, unrestricted in any way.

When we learn that the Real rebuked Ezra for his request concerning Destiny, we recognize that it was a request for this particular kind of awareness, for he sought a capacity regarding what is destined, though that capability is reserved only to Him who has Absolute Being. Thus, Ezra sought that which no creature may experience, nor may even the modalities of things be known save by direct experience. When God said to Ezra, "Unless you desist, I will erase your name from the register of prophets", He meant, "I will remove from you the means to Divine Communication and present things to you as they are manifested, which occur only in terms of your own eternal predisposition, which is the means by which direct perception is experienced. You may perceive only that which you seek to perceive as your eternal predisposition permits. Your predisposition does not permit that you should receive something reserved to God. Although God has given to everything He has created, He has not bestowed on you this particular predisposition. It is not inherent in your creation; had it been so, He who said *He gives to everything He has created* would have given it to you. You should have refrained from such a request of yourself, without requiring a Divine Refusal." Such was God's concern with Ezra, who knew in one way but remained ignorant in another.

God, however, is kind to His servants and has left for them the Universal Prophecy, but that brings no law with it. He has also bestowed on them the power of legislation through the exercise of individual judgement *(ijtihad)* concerning rules and regulations. He has also bequeathed to them the heritage of legislation in the tradition: "The learned are the heirs of the prophets." This inheritance involves the use of individual judgement in certain rulings, which is a form of legislation. When the prophet speaks on matters that lie outside the scope of law, he is speaking as a saint and a gnostic, so that his station as a knower of truth is more complete and perfect than that as an apostle or lawgiver. If you hear any of the Sufis saying or transmitting sayings from him to the effect that saintship is higher than prophecy, he means just this.

THE WISDOM OF PROPHECY IN THE WORD OF JESUS

Al-Hikmat an-Nubuwiyah

From the waters of Mary and the breath of Gabriel,
In the form of a mortal made of clay,
The Spirit was manifested in an essence
Purged of Nature's taint, which is called *sijjin* — 'prison'.
Thus, his sojourn was prolonged,
Enduring, by decree, more than a thousand years.
A spirit from none other than God,
So that he might raise the dead and bring forth birds
    from clay,
And became worthy to be associated with his Lord,
By which he acts in superior and inferior worlds.
God purified him in body and made him transcendent
In the Spirit, the symbol of Divine Creation.*

Spirits have the power of giving life to everything on which they descend. Thus did as-Samiri arrogate to himself some of the influence of the messenger Gabriel, who is a spirit. When he saw that it was Gabriel, and knowing that all he touched would come alive, as-Samiri expropriated some of his power with his own hand and transferred it to the golden calf so that it bellowed. Had he fashioned the calf in another form, it would have made the appropriate sound, like the grumbling of the camel, the bleating of sheep, or even the articulate speech of man.† The measure of life that suffuses a creature is called Divine, and humanity is *al-nasut*, the corporeal form in which the Spirit inheres. Thus, humanity is called a spirit by virtue of *al-lahut*, the

---

* The thousand years refers to the time lapsed since the ascension of Christ and the composition of *The Seals of Wisdom*. The story of Jesus forming birds out of clay is found in the Qur'an and in the apocryphal Gospel known as *Infancy*.

† According to the Qur'an, as-Samiri was the creator of the golden calf the Hebrews worshipped whilst Moses was on Mount Sinai receiving the Ten Commandments.

Divine Nature which inheres in it.

When *ar-ruh al-amin,* the trustworthy spirit which was Gabriel, presented itself to Mary as a perfectly formed human, she imagined that he was an ordinary man who sought carnal pleasures. Accordingly, she sought total refuge from him in God, to be rid of him. Thus she attained to the Divine Presence which is one with *ar-ruh al-ma'nawi,* the Intellectual Spirit. Had Gabriel blown his breath into her at that moment, Jesus would have been born too uncompromising for any to bear because of the state of the mother at the moment. When Gabriel said to her, *I am only a messenger of your Lord, come to give you a pure son,* her anxiety subsided and she relaxed. Then Gabriel blew the spirit of Jesus into her. Gabriel was the vehicle for transmission of the Divine Word to Mary, just as a messenger, *ar-rasul,* transmits His word to his community. God says, *Jesus is His word projected into Mary, and the Spirit from Himself.* Thus did love pervade Mary so that the body of Jesus was created from the actual fluid of Mary and the imaginary water of Gabriel, which was inherent in the moisture of his breath. Breath from the living is moist with water. In this way, the body of Jesus was brought into being from an imaginary and an actual water, appearing in mortal form because his mother was human and Gabriel appeared in human form, since all generation in the human species occurs in this ordinary way.

Jesus came forth to raise the dead because he was a Divine Spirit. Though God alone gives life, the breath itself came from Jesus, just as the breath was from Gabriel, whilst the Word came from God. Jesus actually raised the dead through his breath, just as he himself became manifest from the form of his mother. His raising of the dead, however, was also imaginative, since life emanates from Deity alone. Jesus combines the imaginative and the actual through the reality by which he was created. Bringing the dead to life was attributed to him both actually and in imagination. Concerning the former, it is said, *And He revives the dead,* whilst of the latter, *You will breathe into the clay and it will become a bird by God's permission.*

The humility of Jesus was such that his community was commanded *that they should pay alms completely, humbling themselves,* that if any one of them were struck on one cheek, he should offer also the other, and that he should not strike back in retribution. Jesus took this from his mother, since woman is humble, being under the man, both theoretically and physically. His powers of revival come from the breath of Gabriel in human form. Had Gabriel not come in human form, but in some other, whether animal, plant or mineral, Jesus would have been able to awaken the dead only by assuming that form himself. Had Gabriel appeared in a luminous and incorporeal form, Jesus would not have been able to revive the dead without appearing in that luminous natural form, rather than in the elemental human form deriving from his mother.

It used to be said of him when he revived the dead, "It is he and yet not he." The perception of the observer and the mind of the intelligent man were confused at seeing a mortal man awakening the dead in mind and body. The spectator would be utterly bewildered to see a mortal man performing Divine Acts. Thus, certain people speak of incarnation and say that Jesus is God. Therefore, they are called unbelievers because they practise a form of concealment, since they conceal God, who alone restores the dead in the human form of Jesus. The real error does not lie in their saying "He is God" or "the son of Mary", but in their having abandoned God in favour of a mortal form. Considered in his mortal form, one might say that he is the son of Mary. Considered in his form of humanity, one might say that he is of Gabriel, whilst considered with respect to the revival of the dead, one might say that he is the Spirit of God. Thus, one might call him the Spirit of God, which is to say, life is manifest in whomsoever he breathes. It might be imagined that God is in him, or that an angel is in him, and at other times mortality and humanity. He conforms to that aspect of his reality which predominates in the one who thinks of him. Thus, he is the Word of God, the Spirit of God and the slave of God, and this triple manifestation in sensible form is special to him.

This matter is one that can be known only by direct experience. When Abu Yazid al-Bistami blew on an ant he had killed, it came alive again. At that moment he knew who it was that blew, and in this respect he was like Jesus. Revival by knowledge from spiritual death is the eternal, sublime and luminous Divine Life of which God says, *Who was dead and We made him alive again, and for whom We made a light wherewith to walk amongst men.* One who revives an inert soul with the life of knowledge has thereby truly brought him to life.

> Without Him and but for us,
> That which has become would not be.
> We are servants truly,
> And it is God whom we adore.
> But we are His very Essence.
> When I say Universal Man,
> Do not be deceived by 'man',
> For He has given you a symbol.
> Be divine in essence and a creature in form,
> And you will be, through God, a compassionate one.
> Nourish all creation through Him,
> As He has nourished us also.
> All action is shared
> Between Him and us.
> He who knows by my heart
> Revived it when he gave us life.
> In Him we were existences, essences
> And instances of time.
> In us there is no permanence,
> But it gives us life.

What we have said concerning spiritual breath joining with the elemental mortal form is supported by the Real calling Himself the Compassionate Breath, *an-nafas ar-rahmani*. To attribute a quality is to include everything the quality implies. The breath in one breathing is all that is required to exist. Therefore, the Divine Breath encompasses the cosmic forms, in relation to which it is like the Primordial Substance, *al-jawhar al-hayulani*, being Universal Nature, *at-tabi'ah*. The four elements are a form of Nature, just like that which is superior to them and which they generate, that is, the sublime spirits that are above the seven heavens. The spirits of the seven spheres and their essences derive from the *smoke* the elements generate; they, along with the angels, which come into being from each heaven, are all elemental. These angels are elemental, whilst the superior spirits, *al-mala' al-a'la*, above them are of Universal Nature. It is for this reason that they are described as being in conflict, for Nature itself is self-contradictory. The Breath itself has brought about mutual conflict amongst the Divine

Names, which are relationships. But the Divine Essence is beyond the realm of conflict and is characterized by Self-sufficiency, transcending the Cosmos. Thus, the Cosmos has been established in the form of its Creator which is the Divine Breath.

God kneads human clay in His two hands, which are opposed, although both can be considered right hands. The difference between them is evident, since nothing affects Nature save that which conforms to her polarized nature. When He created Adam with two hands, He called him *bashar*, mortal, human, because of the direct connection, *mubasharah*, suggested by the two hands ascribed to Him. Man's sole superiority over other creatures is in being *bashar*, mortal, for he is superior to all things created without that direct connection, *mubasharah*, with the Divine Presence. Man ranks above the terrestrial and celestial angels, whilst the sublime angels are superior to mankind. Thus, whosoever wishes to know the Divine Breath must first know the Cosmos. "Who knows himself, knows his Lord", who is manifest in him. The Cosmos is manifested in the Divine Breath through which God relieved the Divine Names from the distress they experienced by the non-manifestation of their effects. The first effect of the Breath is experienced only in the Divine Presence, and thereafter descends through universal release, down to the least thing to be created.

Jesus said, *Worship God.* He used the name *Allah* because there are many kinds of worshippers, many acts of worship and different religious traditions. He does not use any specific name but only that name which embraces them all. Then he said, *My Lord and your Lord,* since His relationship as Lord with one creature is not the same as with another. When he says, *only what you commanded me to say,* Jesus lays the stress on himself as one who is commanded, which constitutes his servanthood, since a command is only given to one who, it is supposed, will comply, whether he does so in fact or not. Since the command descends through the hierarchy of ranks, everything manifested in a particular rank is affected by what is afforded it by the reality of that rank. The rank of the ordered has a discipline that is apparent in everything ordered, just as the rank of commanding has a discipline apparent in everyone who commands. When God says, *Establish prayer,* He is the commander, the one who obliges and the commanded. But when the servant prays, *O my Lord, forgive me!* he is the commander, whilst the Real is the commanded, for what God requires of His servant by His command is identical with that which the servant requires of the Real by his command. Thus, every supplication is invariably responded to, even if it seems to be delayed. Response is inevitable, even if only by intention.

When God makes a servant fly to give expression to some matter, He does so only that He might respond to him and fulfil his need. Therefore, let no one think that what he has been made fit for is late in coming. Rather, let him emulate the zeal of God's Messenger, in all his states, so that he may hear with his inner or outer ear, or in whatever way God may cause him to hear His response. If God blesses you with an orally expressed request, He will cause you to hear His response with the physical ear, but if He blesses you with an inner request, then He will cause you to hear His response inwardly.

OM

GLOSSARY

al'Abd	Servant; symbolically, a mystic devotee of the Divine
'Adam	Immutably unmanifest; the Void
Adam Kadmon	In the Qabbalah, the Archetypal Man, the heavenly prototype of Man and Nature
Adh-dhat	The essence or quiddity; that to which all qualities of a thing are referred
Adh-dhawq	Men of spiritual inclination; the faculty of intuition
al-'Adl	The Just, a Divine Name
al-'Afuw	Approving; the Pardoner, a Divine Name
al-Ahad	The One, a Divine Name; in Sufi thought, *al-ahadiyah* is Supreme Unity and the state of uttermost absorption in the Divine
Ahl-al-haqaïq	The Divine Realities
al-Akhir	The Last, a Divine Name
'Alem al-khayal	Realm of the creative imagination
'Alem al-mithal	World of analogies, which corresponds to *'alem al-khayal*
al-Ali	The Elevated, the Most High, a Divine Name
Allah	Literally, God; the primary of the Divine Names
Amr	Divine Order; the Divine Command, symbolized by the word of creation, *kun,* 'Be!'
al-Asma al-husna	Infinite in number; the Names of Beauty or the Divine Names
al-Awwal	The First, a Divine Name
al-A'yan	Eternal essences; the unchanging archetypes
al-'Ayn	Latent essence; the source
al-Azal	The One without Beginning; eternity
Baqa	Immortality in Deity
Barzakh	Bridge; symbolically, the link between two degrees of existence
Bashar	Mortal man
al-Batin	Inner, unmanifest, hidden, a Divine Name
Binah	Intelligence; the third *Sephira* of the Sephirothal Tree in the Qabbalah

Chesed	Love, Mercy; the fourth *Sephira* of the Sephirothal Tree in the Qabbalah
Chokmah	Wisdom, the second *Sephira* of the Sephirothal Tree in the Qabbalah
Fana	The passing of the individual self into universal Being; renunciation of all desires
al-Fayd	Inexhaustible afflatus; the overflowing of Infinite Being
al-Furqan	Discrimination; revelation in general as *shari'a*, law
Fusus	Seals; settings for gems; bezels
al-Ghaffar	The Forgiver, a Divine Name
al-Ghafur	All-Forgiving, a Divine Name
Hadarat al-ghayb al-mudafi	The Divine Presence in the Unmanifest
Hadarat al-ghayb al-mutlaq	The Divine Presence in the Absolute and Unknowable
al-Hadarat al-jam 'iyah	Divine Presence in its impartite integrity; see *hadarat*
Hadarat al-khayal	The Divine Presence in the realm of imagination
Hadarat ash-shahadat al-mutlaqah	The Divine Presence in the manifest
Hadith	Traditional saying of Muhammad handed down outside the Qur'an through known intermediaries
al-Hakam	The Judge, a Divine Name
al-Hamid	The Adored, the Praiseworthy, a Divine Name
Haqiqat al-haqaïq	The Reality of Realities; the highest Logos; the intangible *barzakh* between Divinity and manifestation
al-Haqq	The One Reality; the Truth; the Real, a Divine Name
al-Haybah	Reverent awe; the contrary of *al-uns*
al-Hikam	Wisdom
al-Himmah	Conscious power of impressing ideas on the cosmos; spiritual will; the ardent turning of the soul towards the Divine
al-Huwiyah	The Supreme Self

al-Ihsan	Spiritual vision; spiritual virtue
Ijtihad	Individual judgement
Ilah	Divinity; hence Allah *(al-Ilah)*
Imam	Leader, especially in prayer
Insan	Man
al-Insan al-kabir	The Great Man, the macrocosm; *cf., Adam Kadmon*
al-Insan al-kamil	The Universal Man; the archetypal human being and the perfected man who has realized all degrees of being
al-Iradah	Wish
Islam	Surrender; submission
Isti'dad	Predisposition, receptivity
al-Jabbar	Establisher of Order; the Omnipotent, a Divine Name
al-Jam'iyat al-ilahiyah	Divine synthesis
Jasad	Subtle form
al-Jawhar al-hayulani	Primordial substance
Jihad	Holy war
al-Kamal	The infinitude in which all realities are immersed; Divine plenitude
Kashf	Vision; instinctual intuition; the withdrawing of a veil
Kathif	Gross; corporeal; *cf., latif*
al-Kawmu khayal	'The world is Imagination'
Kether	The Crown; the first *Sephira* of the Sephirothal Tree in the Qabbalah
Khalifah	The Representative of the Divine
Khalil Allah	Intimate Friend of Allah
al-Khaliq	The Creator, a Divine Name
Khatim al-awliya	Seal of the saints
Khatim ar-rasul	Seal of the messengers
al-Khayal	Creative imagination
al-Lahut	The Divine Nature inherent in humanity
Latif	Subtle; fine; *cf., kathif*

Majmu	The Totality
al-Makan	Cosmic locus
Maqamat	Divine Stations or Names through which the Divine Essence is manifest
al-Mashi'ah	Will
al-Mishkat	Niche, tabernacle
Mubasharah	Direct connection; that which makes one happy
Mumkinat	Possibilities, distinguished from necessities and contingencies
al-Muntaqim	Wrathful; the Avenger, a Divine Name
Nabi	Prophet
an-Nabi	The Prophet
an-Nafas ar-rahmani	Compassionate Breath; the manifesting principle of the Divine
an-Nafs	The individual soul; in contrast to *ruh*, spirit, it is the separative self
an-Nafs al wahidah	Single spiritual essence, the source of individual souls
al-Nasut	The corporeal form in which Spirit inheres; human nature
an-Nur	The Light, a Divine Name
al-Qabid	The Restrictor, a Divine Name
Qabil	Pure receptacle; passive substance
Qada'	Decree
Qadar	Destiny
Qadasa	Holiness
al-Qahhar	The Victorious, a Divine Name
al-Qalb	The Heart; the faculty of pure intuition
Qiblah	Appropriate direction; ritual orientation
al-Qidam	The Ancient of Days; eternity
al-Qur'an	Literally, recitation; in Sufi symbolism, immediate illumination, revelation as knowledge; the Self as a united totality; the name of the sacred scripture of Islam
Qutb al-arifin	The axis of true knowledge

Rabb	Lord; Deity in respect to man
Rabbur ul-'alam	Guide of the world
Rahmah	Compassion; pure mercy
al-Rahman	The Compassionate, the Beneficent, a Divine Name
Ramadan	Ninth month of the lunar year, requiring total abstinence from food and drink during the daylight and only light refreshment after dark
ar-Ruh al-amin	Trustworthy spirit; a name of the archangel Gabriel
al-Ruh al-ma'nawi	The Intellectual Spirit
Ru'ya	Vision
Sephiroth	The ten centres of creative light constituting the tree of manifestation in the Qabbalah; literally, numbers, centres; emanations
Shahada	The word of witness, the Muslim profession of faith; 'There is no God but Allah; Muhammad is his prophet'
Shari'a	Traditional law
Sijjin	Prison; in the Qur'an, *sijjin* refers to the inferior worlds
Sirr	Mystery, secret; in Sufi symbolism, the centre of consciousness
at-Tabi'ah	Universal Nature
at-Tajalli	Self-unveiling; Divine irradiation
Tanfis	To give relief
al-Tanzih	Transcendental understanding; withdrawal
Taqlib	Turning
Tasha'ub	Innumerable ramifications
al-Tashbih	Understanding mediated by analogy; affirmation
'Ubudiyah	Unwavering servitude; quality of the perfect servant
Uluhiyah	Divinity; the Divine Nature as a quality of Deity
al-Umar al-kulliyah	Universal ideas; archetypal realities
Umma	Community
al-Uns	Confiding intimacy; the contrary of *al-haybah*

Wahdat al-wujud	The Oneness of Being
al-Wahhab	The Bestower, the Giver, a Divine Name
al-Wahi	Divine inspiration
al-Wahid	The Unique, a Divine Name
al-Wahm	Illusion; conjecture; opinion
Wali	Saint
al-Wali	The Friend; the Ruler, a Divine Name
al-Wasi'	The All-Encompassing, the Vast, a Divine Name
al-Wujud	Beyond the aroma of manifest existence; the One
al-Zahir	The Manifest, the Apparent, a Divine Name; contrasted with *al-batin,* the Hidden

THE PYTHAGOREAN SANGHA

THE JEWEL IN THE LOTUS edited by Raghavan Iyer
THE GRIHASTHA ASHRAMA by B. P. Wadia
THE MORAL AND POLITICAL THOUGHT
   OF MAHATMA GANDHI by Raghavan Iyer

THE MAITREYA ACADEMY

PARAPOLITICS — TOWARD THE CITY OF MAN by Raghavan Iyer
THE PLATONIC QUEST by E. J. Urwick
OBJECTIVITY AND CONSCIOUSNESS by Robert Rein'l

SANGAM TEXTS

THE BEACON LIGHT by H. P. Blavatsky
THE SERVICE OF HUMANITY by D. K. Mavalankar
HIT THE MARK by W. Q. Judge
THE PROGRESS OF HUMANITY by A. P. Sinnett
CONSCIOUSNESS AND IMMORTALITY by T. Subba Row
THE GATES OF GOLD by M. Collins
THE LANGUAGE OF THE SOUL by R. Crosbie
THE ASCENDING CYCLE by G. W. Russell
THE DOCTRINE OF THE BHAGAVAD GITA by Bhavani Shankar
THE LAW OF SACRIFICE by B. P. Wadia

SACRED TEXTS

RETURN TO SHIVA (from the *Yoga Vasishtha Maharamayana*)

THE GATHAS OF ZARATHUSTRA — The Sermons of Zoroaster

TAO TE CHING by Lao Tzu

SELF-PURIFICATION (Jaina Sutra)

THE DIAMOND SUTRA (from the Final Teachings of the Buddha)

THE GOLDEN VERSES OF PYTHAGORAS
  (with the commentary of Hierocles)

IN THE BEGINNING — The Mystical Meaning of Genesis

THE GOSPEL ACCORDING TO THOMAS
  (with complementary texts)

THE SEALS OF WISDOM — The Essence of Islamic Mysticism
  by Ibn al-'Arabi

CHANTS FOR CONTEMPLATION by Guru Nanak

INSTITUTE OF WORLD CULTURE

THE SOCIETY OF THE FUTURE by Raghavan Iyer

THE RELIGION OF SOLIDARITY by Edward Bellamy

THE BANQUET (Percy Bysshe Shelley's translation
  of Plato's *Symposium*)

THE DREAM OF RAVAN *A Mystery*

THE LAW OF VIOLENCE AND THE LAW OF LOVE by Leo Tolstoy

THE RECOVERY OF INNOCENCE by Pico Iyer

UTILITARIANISM AND ALL THAT by Raghavan Iyer

NOVUS ORDO SECLORUM by Raghavan Iyer

The CGP emblem identifies this book as a production of Concord Grove Press, publishers since 1975 of books and pamphlets of enduring value in a format based upon the Golden Ratio. This volume was typeset in Journal Roman Bold, and Bodoni Bold, printed and softbound by Sangam Printers. A list of publications can be obtained from Concord Grove Press, P.O. Box 959, Santa Barbara, California 93102, U.S.A.